ON THE NEWS
...IN THE NEWS

ON THE NEWS
...IN THE NEWS

A Journalist's Own Story of Recovery and Self-Discovery

JOHN BOEL

ISBN 978-1-935497-44-8

Printed in Canada

PUBLISHED BY

Butler Books
P.O. Box 7311
Louisville, KY 40207
phone: (502) 897-9393
fax: (502) 897-9797
www.butlerbooks.com

DEDICATION

This book is dedicated to my wife Brenda,
who shows me the meaning of unconditional love every day.

My daughters Kelsey and Brianna,
who blossom every day in ways I never imagined.

My parents Jim and Susan, who continue to do
whatever it takes to put me in a position to succeed
at every opportunity I want to pursue in life.

My grandfather John, who showed me the importance of
recording important thoughts and moments in our lives,
which I would later learn is a craft called journalism.

My college journalism advisor Henry,
who taught me I can always do better than my best.

My friend Erin, who demonstrates how the people we overlook
in life may be the ones who contribute most when we need it.

My dorm mates in rehab who, in the worst month of
their lives, showed me a depth of compassion, honesty
and love I had never experienced before.

My publisher Carol, who encouraged me at a low point in my life
to turn the lessons I've learned into a book so I may help others.

Racism 75
Public Park Pleasure 77
In the Name of God 81
Security Breach 85
White Boy in the Hood 89
Troy Story 93
Good Evening, I'm Ron Burgundy? . . . 97
Lethal Dejection 103
A Man of Iron 107

IN THE NEWS

Institutionalized 113
Celebrity Rehab Without Dr. Drew . . 117
Revelations 121
Family Matters 125
Popular Culture 131
The Adjustment Bureau 133
Done-Employment Office 139
Hypocrisy 143
An Angel 147
Anything Goes 151
Paging Dr. Phil 155
Life in the Slow Lane 159
East End Househusband 163
Judgment Day 167
Grounded 173
The Finish Line 177
Unscripted Moment 185

FOREWORD

Question: How do you know when your life has hit the skids?

Answer: When a TV reporter contacts you and requests an interview.

Yes, there is a chance it's going to be a positive story. But 99 times out of 100, it's not going to be good.

How do I know? Because I've been doing it for more than a quarter of a century. Stroking, schmoozing, sometimes shamelessly working people for interviews at the worst moments of their lives. You know Don Henley's song line: "Get the widow on the set; we need dirty laundry."

Today, my life came full circle. The dirtiest laundry on the clothesline is mine. A big, embarrassing pair of soiled underwear flapping in the breeze for all to see. People can't seem to get enough of my dirty laundry because when I wasn't publicly tattling on people as a news anchor, I was taking down bad guys as an investigative reporter. After my second DUI in two years, a surreal termination, and a month-long stay in rehab, one of my rival Louisville news anchors asks me if she can be the one to "share" my story.

No. I'd rather tell my own story. In fact, I have many stories to tell—from the people I met and lessons I learned while I was *on* the news—to the people I met and lessons

I learned while I was *in* the news. Outrageous stories. Disgusting stories. Sad stories. Courage from people and places no one expected. Inspiration from unlikely sources. Comical ironies in the television news business. And painful stories after I've been handed a "reporter involvement" assignment that sends me places where no one wants to go.

All journalists are taught to tell both sides of the TV news story. Few journalists have lived and learned from both sides of the TV news spotlight as I have.

ON THE NEWS
...IN THE NEWS

I'm a top story on my station's website, with my mug shot displayed as well. And the anchors I work with are reading my arrest story right there in the same newscast segments with the day's murder and mayhem.

There are, on average, about 100 drunk driving arrests every day in the Commonwealth of Kentucky. But when the anchorman gets one, it's the uncommon talk of the town. Google my name two days later and 243 different websites have posted my story, from Memphis to MSNBC. I'm suddenly learning what it's like to be on the other side of the news stories I do every day.

"What's more embarrassing, having your mug shot broadcast for being arrested for DUI, or having your own news organization report it?"

That's the lead to one of the Internet stories. Another one names me "Mug Shot of the Year." Below most of them are forums where people can anonymously lob hate bombs at me. They stack up by the dozens with people who hope I get fired. People who've lost loved ones to drunk drivers. People who hope my two daughters are disgraced by even the mention of my name. Based on what they write, I can tell some of them are fellow Louisville journalists. Emailers who claim they are cops threaten to follow me until they catch me again. That's nothing new. They've been doing that for years. Louisville is a very small big city.

TV is unwatchable now. State police just bought a bunch of air time to push their latest drunk driving crackdown. It seems like there's a drunk driving commercial in every break, on every station. And I feel like I'm starring in every one.

The hate rains down so hard, I try to escape to my parents' house in Wisconsin. But walleye fishing in my favorite spot in the world at the peak of fall color doesn't relieve my guilt at all. I spent most of my life in the cheese state but never realized until now the prominence of alcohol in every facet of life here. Baseball fans cheer for the Brewers. Every gas station at interstate exits has single cans of beer on ice in mouth-watering vats right up at the cash registers. They are begging for us to drink and drive. Beer bongs are for sale, too, in the checkout lines. Taverns outnumber all the other stores combined in small towns. My final exam for one college writing class was in a bar. Parents bring their kids to the bars. They even set infants up on the bar, in baby carriers, with baby formula bottles next to the beer bottles. I need to leave this place as fast as possible.

When I get back to Louisville, I only leave the house on Halloween, when I can wear a mask as I escort my nine year old around. I take pills to go to sleep at night. I wake up hoping it's all a bad dream. The ritual continues for weeks.

That's a lot of time to think about all the people who've been subjects of stories I've read, or investigations I've done. In only a handful of cases have I ever felt sorry for any of them. I did feel bad about the car wash workers we caught in a hidden camera sting stealing money and jewelry from cars. They got fired and embarrassed publicly when they could have been making more money collecting unemployment. I eventually felt bad about showing the dozens of people we caught stealing items donated to charities like Goodwill and Salvation Army. Many of them were dirt poor and really needed those things. My coworkers stressed, in both cases, they were stealing items that didn't belong to them. But somehow it didn't make me feel any better.

I got into an argument with a relative a long time ago about his small town newspaper publishing every name involved in every crime. Every shoplifting. Every DUI. Every pot possession. He was outraged at how hard they tried to publicly humiliate everyone who does anything wrong. I had no problem with it. I know people gobble that stuff up, skipping past the front page news. Besides, if you don't want to be embarrassed, don't break the law.

Now I'm seeing it from the other side. How many times per day have I read stories with a mug shot over my shoulder? Probably five, minimum. That's 100 a month, and more than 1,000 per year. No wonder so many people are lining up to dance on my grave. Why do people love hearing about other people screwing up so much? I never thought about it before. Maybe it makes us feel better about ourselves.

The first time I pick up a newspaper in Louisville after my arrest, it's already out with a year-ender story entitled "The 10 Biggest Losers of 2008." I am number three. Then, a photo gets out of Olympic hero Michael Phelps hitting a bong at a party. He just won eight gold medals in the most amazing athletic performance of my lifetime. But now, no one remembers his achievement. One bong hit trumps eight gold medals. One DUI trumps 62 Emmy awards. That's just the way it is.

Magazines are arriving at my house, along with the payment invoices. Problem is, I didn't order any of them.

Somebody who knows my address is playing a trick on me. The address on the magazine subscriptions is correct. But the name of the person who lives here is now listed as "John Beer." The only place in the world I can go to feel better about myself, no matter what I've done, is church. Sent home from my job, despised by viewers, and ashamed to even look in the mirror, I need to hear something encouraging. But instead I learn I am being suspended from my volunteer position serving communion each week. My minister explains a church visitor in the pew may well recognize the guy serving communion as the DUI guy recently on the news. I'm even an embarrassment to my own church. That's hard to do, especially amid all that stuff about Jesus and forgiveness. So I try to stay away, even on Sundays, making up excuses as often as I can.

A crisis like this leaves me with a lot of time to look back on my life. Flipping through my journal, I see it was 25 years ago this month when I picked up a TV camera for the first time to go shoot a story. Skinny tie. Bad porn moustache. Had to lop off the permed mullet for the first college newscast.

Happy 25th anniversary. As a journalist, I've grown exponentially with all I've experienced since my college days. As a person, I haven't matured at all.

ON THE NEWS

INITIATION

Falling over ourselves to get the best shot

It's the first big shoot of my life. The first time I've ever gone out of town with the gear. Somehow, I manage to convince my college advisor and the dean to let me have my own outdoors show for a semester. My first episode is going to cover The American Birkebeiner, the largest and longest cross-country ski race in North America. More than eight thousand people attempt the 34-mile event each year. I don't cross-country ski, but I love the shot in the opening of "Wide World of Sports" that shows a sea of eight thousand skiers starting the race.

I have no idea how much work is involved in planning, shooting, writing, editing, and post-producing a half-hour show, but I'm an aggressive college kid with big dreams, and now a big camera in my hand. I'm in tiny Cable, Wisconsin, shooting a show that airs on cable TV in Eau Claire, but I'm surrounded by sports guys from the big time TV markets of Minneapolis and Milwaukee, as well as the network TV crews. In fact, there are so many media crews here to get the money shot of the race start, they've erected two giant media platforms at the start line.

Perhaps it's first-time jitters. Perhaps it's my competitiveness. I'm the first one there in the morning so I can ascend the 12-foot-high platform and get the pole position. I set my tripod and camera up on the front left corner, where I'll have the best, unobstructed shot of skiers taking off and passing me to my left. That turns out to be key, because both platforms are overflowing more than a half-hour before starting time, and 80 percent of them have a lousy view.

My watch is set down to the second with the official race clock. There is no countdown to the start. A cannon is fired at 8 A.M. and then everybody shuffles off. I'm shivering with anticipation and without anti-freeze as I look out on the brightly colored ski jackets and hats stretching back as far as the eye can see. It's not easy to cover the Birkebeiner. As soon as the race goes off, we have to hustle to the nearby idling media buses, which will hurriedly drive us to various points along the 34-mile route as we try to keep up with the world's fastest cross-country skiers.

At 7:58, I start rolling my tape on the mass of humanity, fully fueled and ready to take off. Can't miss the cannon blast. At t-minus 30 seconds to blast off, with about 30 photographers around me talking, laughing and adjusting their apertures, a strange sound is getting louder. I've only heard it once before, when I fell through the ice on a frozen lake.

The long groan I hear is not from ice or people. The wooden supports on the media platform are moaning as they buckle and snap under all the weight of overweight, overdressed photographers. My eye is focused on the race through my camera viewfinder, but the sinking feeling in my stomach tells me we're going down. The shrieks and screams sound just like kids on a plummeting roller coaster.

I'm one of the last to go because I'm way up in the front corner position, which is directly above the last support to give way. So my backward free-fall landing is cushioned by all the people and planks that crashed ahead of me. As I lie there clutching my camera, looking straight up into the sky trying to figure out what just happened, the cannon erupts. Thousands of skis are whooshing past my head as the American Birkebeiner is underway. No one stops to help. They can't. They'll be crushed by the crowd if they do.

The moaning and crying in the media pile drowns out the race noise anyway. I'm last one down, so I'm first one off. The woman I landed on has broken ribs. EMS is quickly on the scene, but there are many broken bones to be attended to. A quick inventory of my wounds reveals two puncture holes in my pants directly over the part of my body that procreates. I'm too young to be gelded. Fortunately for me, those nails went in at an angle and pierced deep into my thigh.

Still stunned for several minutes, I limp into the nearest building so I can call my advisor at school.

"Henry, this is John Boel. Sorry to bother you but I've been involved in a bad accident here at the Birkebeiner. The media platform collapsed with a lot of people on it."

His response?

"Is the gear okay?"

Good question. I haven't thought of that yet. I was worried about the blood running down my leg and the other injured people. When I fire everything up, it appears to be working. So, I run to the media bus, where there are plenty of good seats available. One of the guys offers to check my gear out further to make sure it's okay.

"Hey, do you realize you were rolling when everything crashed down? It never shut off, and you got a great shot of it all as it happened?"

Wow, never thought of that.

"You're gonna make a lot of money off this tape. What you shot is incredible."

I will learn many more times in my career that it's better to be lucky than good.

UNLUCKY NUMBER SEVEN

Some stories are too sad for words.

I t is quite literally the saddest, most surreal scene I've ever witnessed: seven hearses lined up. Huge white snowflakes floating down as seven white caskets are wheeled out of a funeral. Most of them are mini-caskets because they hold the bodies of small children.

This can't be happening. The most beautiful snowfall I've ever witnessed is trying to mask the most gut-wrenching moment I've ever covered as a journalist. The story behind it makes it even worse.

As a new reporter, fresh out of college, all I know when my boss sends me out is a single mom and six of her children have died in a fire. One of the kids is still alive. It happens right before Christmas. The charred Christmas tree in the blackened snow outside of the gutted house gives me a hint at the cause.

I find out where the mother worked. I walk in the doughnut shop where she worked the counter. Her grieving co-worker pulls herself out of her tears long enough to tell me a far worse tear-jerker. The single mother was trying to raise seven children without child support. Her heat had been cut off because she couldn't keep up with the bills on her counter worker pay from the doughnut shop.

Somehow, she managed to scrape up in tips the 25 dollars needed to make the minimum payment that would get her heat turned back on, at least until she couldn't pay the next bill. But the day she had to go to the power company and make that payment also happened to be her five-year-old daughter's birthday. She decided to spend the money on a couple of birthday presents for the little girl instead of restoring their heat. That night, after a happier birthday, a space heater keeping the poor family warm ignited the Christmas tree. The Christmas tree ignited the home.

Two days later, as the hearses whisk the white caskets away to a burial, a blinding white snowstorm tries to bury this horrible ending. Across the street with the other reporters, I wonder what it must be like to try to support seven kids on a doughnut shop worker wage. I try to imagine what it's like to choose between heat for your family and your five-year-old's birthday. I wonder what life is going to be like for the eight-year-old boy who survived this American family tragedy.

A few years later, I watch the parents of seven children rush to the scene of a Fourth of July house fire and crumble into a wailing heap as they learn that all seven kids died. Their bodies are found stacked up at the doorways. It turns out the mom who lived there locked the doors from the outside and went down the block to party with neighbors. Her power had been turned off as well and one of the candles she was using to light the house instead lit a fire. The screaming, trapped children suffered a horrible death.

Two similar tragedies. Same death tolls. Both trace back to actions by mothers. One mother was selfless. One mother was selfish. The selfless mom is with her kids. The selfish mom has to live with herself now.

captures everything beautifully on tape. Faces, pickup truck license number, everything.

The sting captain I'm riding with asks to view the tape. He studies it for a few seconds, then his head drops, and he sets the camera down in disbelief. It takes a few minutes for me to get the real story out of him.

The road hunters who got away are the same three friends he had mentioned who had been hunting all morning on his farm. The men who shot at the fake deer along the road are guys who knew the captain was running a fake deer road hunting sting not far away. One is a state trooper. One is the local jailer. They were taking a break and heading to town for lunch when they saw that big, brawny buck standing out in the field. There's something about seeing a buck or a bird through a gun scope that makes grown men lose their minds.

I feel terrible about having to confront those guys for the TV report, because I remember road hunting so well. At least my dad shot at real birds.

KNOCK, KNOCK

A lesson in forgiveness

You never know how it will turn out. Somebody dies. It's a high-profile news story. So, reporters are sent out to knock on doors where people are mourning dead people. Try to get an interview, or at least a photo. By far, the worst part of the news business. One of my reporter friends got so sick of it, he quit. On the one hand, it often becomes exploitation of grief. On the other hand, some viewers care about the tragic things that happen to people. I know if it happened to me, I would like someone to say something kind about my life. But I understand why people slam doors on us at the worst times of their lives.

A mother glares at me through the front window the morning after an unbelievable chain of events. A guy who had stalked and raped her daughter managed to bond out of jail without anyone notifying the family. The rapist promptly fired seven shots into her daughter's head and chest as she was leaving work on her 21st birthday. Happy birthday. There is a reporter pounding on the door looking for a photo and an interview.

A barefoot family, in a rural county, chases us with guns

any parable in the Bible. When he finishes, grown men around me are crying. But a smile stretches across my sleepy face. I finally get it. This is one case where nobody in the media is going to exploit the family of a victim of tragedy. This time, the family member is using the media, and every other avenue possible, to get his message across. A great message. A great man.

As proud as fathers can be of their daughters, I bet Walt's pretty daughters are pretty proud of their dad.

YOUR STANDARD MASSACRE

Why the gun control debate may never be solved

They happen all the time now. Workplace shooting sprees. School shootings. Shopping mall massacres. But in 1989, it's a different story. Not a lot of crazed gunmen walking into work with duffle bags full of guns. The term "going postal" is not yet coined, let alone common. Metal detectors are mostly used by nerds in Speedos searching for coins on the beach.

On September 14, a man named Joseph Wesbecker takes Louisville right to the top of the workplace shooting lists. Our country has never really been the same since.

I get the call in the middle of the most hellacious week of news coverage I've ever experienced. From Western Kentucky one day, where 10 men die in a mine collapse, to Eastern Kentucky, where a young gunman takes his whole class hostage, it's now Louisville's turn to keep the network news crews parked in the Bluegrass.

They are wheeling bullet-riddled bodies out of the Standard Gravure printing plant downtown. They are discovering Louisville doesn't have enough gurneys for something like this. And my bosses can't call in enough people to cover such a staggering story.

Forty-seven-year-old Joe Wesbecker must have watched *The Terminator*. The former Standard Gravure worker strolls in the main entrance with an AK-47, two MAC-11s, a 9mm pistol, a .38 caliber revolver, and hundreds of rounds of ammunition. He shoots the first person he sees. The receptionist never has a chance. Neither does anyone else. A printing plant is loud. So loud, it covers the popping sound of the assault rifle as Wesbecker calmly walks the hallways, searching for the managers, but shooting almost everyone he sees. He hands out only one excused absence, with a bizarre comment to a pressman who clearly had done something favorable for Joe once upon a time.

"I told them I'd be back. Get away from me."

No one else Wesbecker encounters is spared. Not even one of his friends. He actually apologizes to his bleeding body. It's hard to tell who you're murdering when you shoot 'em in the back.

Wesbecker never does find a boss. He shoots 20 people, killing eight, before terminating himself with the 9mm. The worst part of the story comes afterward, in numerous interviews, where coworkers reveal that Joe had been boasting about getting even and wiping out the place for a year because he was outraged at how he had been treated there. But for me, the most intruiging part of the Standard Gravure massacre comes in relationships I develop with two of the survivors.

Mike Campbell's version of the shooting spree is the most chilling. He is sitting in the break-room with six other workers when he sees the muzzle of an assault rifle peeking into the room. It's the only way in or out. They are trapped. "Pop, pop, pop."

As people dive under tables, Wesbecker systematically shoots each person three times. He even shoots down through the table tops to get at the terrified coworkers. Out of ammo, he steps outside to reload. Mike resigns himself to death as Wesbecker comes back in with a second serving for everyone. But somehow, Campbell does not die. Hit four times, he waits for death but it never arrives. He later learns that they were the last ones shot, as Wesbecker then stepped out of the break-room and killed himself.

Jackie Miller is a different story. She is among the first to encounter the crazed gunman. She figures out what is going on right away and runs to her purse to try to get her gun before he gets her. She is reaching for her .38 in her office when Wesbecker walks in and sprays four bullets into her body.

Two survivors, shot four times each. Two workers rendered painfully disabled for the rest of their lives, despite dozens of surgeries. Two of the finest people I've ever met. But while one goes on a gun control crusade after the massacre, the other decorates her wheelchair with NRA stickers.

Mike Campbell insists there is no reason why anyone, much less a crazy person like Joe Wesbecker, should be walking around with all those weapons. He says AK-47 assault rifles are for war, not pheasant hunting, and we are

camera recorded people pouring in money, no questions asked.

"So, you just want me to go out and rip off that story?"

"Yes, it'll be great."

Reporters get mad when they're assigned stories that have already been done in the newspaper or on another TV station. When I complained long ago to a news director about this, he said, "John, there's something you have to realize about this business. There are no new stories in TV news, just new ways of doing the same things." That turned out to be an accurate observation.

So, I suit up, string a hidden microphone under my fake beard, and position my photographer up in a parking garage across the street from a busy downtown street corner. I place a large, gift-wrapped box at my feet. Before my photographer can get a white-balance off of my white beard, people passing by start launching money at me. No one asks where the money is going. I have no sign indicating the name of a charity or anything about this collection effort. I never ask anyone for a donation. I don't even look like a plausible Santa. But I'm making it rain dollars.

My unknown charity is not registered, and I'm not complying with any of the laws on street corner fundraising, but police drive by and wave. Now it's time to engage the happy holiday contributors.

"Excuse me, you just gave me a lot of money, but you never asked where it's going."

"Well, sh--, yer Santa Claus, ain't ya?"

Simple, effective logic. Others say they assume it's going

to a good cause. After one hour, I have a lot of money, but no one asks who is going to receive it. One guy does ask me a question.

"Hey, Santa, you know what I want for Christmas? A babe, under the tree, just layin' there with no clothes on. Maybe just wrapped in a little bit of ribbon."

He has no idea a hidden camera and microphone are picking up every bit of his perverted Christmas fantasy. And he has no idea that while other reporters would not include this in their story, I will absolutely work it in.

As we're getting ready to wrap up and rush back to put something on the air, a homeless-looking guy walks up. He smells drunk. He sounds drunk. Wow, this'll be good. Even a homeless guy is going to dig down and contribute to the needy. But instead of making a deposit, he wants to make a withdrawal.

"Can you spare me some change?"

"No, I can't." I realize this is one situation where I have to explain where the money is really going.

"This money is going for the Toys for Tots program. You know, needy kids."

Problem is, he's needy. He's intoxicated. And he sees money. He helps himself to a big scoop of cash and takes off down the street. I've been robbed by an unarmed, drunken, homeless man.

The crime is caught on surveillance camera. My photographer was rolling, in more ways than one. We put the thief on TV, too. But he is never apprehended. And, as usual, I'm ripped in the media.

"John Boel: Santa Slayer" is the headline. According to a local media critic, I've destroyed Santa Claus and I've damaged charitable giving by doing that story.

Like most people, he doesn't realize I'm just following orders. Or maybe people think I like dressing up like Santa. After all, news anchors do wear makeup.

THE PEDO-FILES

It's easy to catch a predator

In 1994, this Internet thing is pretty new. Chat rooms are in vogue. And pedophilia is apparently booming. The investigative reporter at our sister station in Orlando just posed online as a 13-year-old boy, and he captured a trucker driving there, from several states away, to try to have sex with the kid. My boss wants me to replicate this unbelievable undercover sting. Chris Hansen and "Dateline" won't be catching predators for another ten years. I'm among the first in the country to try this. Problem is, I don't even know how to sign onto a computer.

When I finally figure out how to get in a chat room and post a profile of a 13-year-old boy, we can't get the camera fired up fast enough. Within seconds, I can't keep up with the dozens of old men pouncing on what they believe is a young boy. I'm conversing with coaches, teachers and scout leaders. I'm doing a poor job of acting like a kid under siege, because I'm freaking out about all of this.

Before I began, I talked to a detective to get some guidance on "entrapment." He told me as long as I don't suggest or offer any sexual activity, I can say whatever I want. This really never becomes an issue, because without any urging, they describe in great detail exactly what they're going to do to me when they meet me in Louisville.

The report done in Orlando had one glaring problem. When the Internet predator arrived at the meeting place, the reporter and photographer jumped out of their vehicle and peppered the guy with questions. He was able to lie his way out of it with various excuses, because he never actually approached anyone. So, my bosses agree with my request to hire a legal adult, who looks very young, to sit there with a hidden microphone and play the role of the 13-year-old boy. It sounds impossible but we quickly find a local 18-year-old youth minister who actually looks that young and is willing to do it.

It takes five minutes to find someone willing to drive to Louisville to have sex with a 13-year-old boy. My fingers are shaking on the keyboard as an Indianapolis ambulance driver named Will even books a motel for the day.

I've never really been good at confrontational interviews. Half the time, I feel bad for ruining the person's life. And to be honest, I get nervous in these situations. Multiply that feeling times 100 while I'm sitting in our surveillance van across the street from the Seneca Park bathroom. Our actor with no experience is also a nervous wreck. He wants to know what to say and do. I tell him to just get the guy talking. We'll roll tape and listen in as long as we can, and then jump out and confront him.

"If the guy tries to abduct you at gunpoint, just run."

Nobody thinks that's funny. But police turned down my

request to work with us on this sting. We'll just have to rely on the fact that pedophiles are normally not violent. I've had some out-of-body experiences in my life. The births of my daughters. Walking down the wedding aisle. Finishing the Ironman Triathlon. But nothing comes close to the feeling that sweeps over me when a blonde guy matching Will's description pulls in with Indianapolis license plates. He walks right up to our actor and starts some awkward small talk. It's going very badly. I'm afraid he's going to realize this is a pathetic sting attempt and bolt, so we jump out and confront him.

Trembling badly, I don't know what to say. He doesn't try to flee like I thought he would. He sits right there and answers every feeble question.

"You came here to have sex with what you thought was a 13-year-old."

"No I didn't, sir. I came here to spend the day in Louisville."

"You rented a motel room."

"Yes, to spend the day in Louisville, sir."

I do an extremely poor job of cross-examining his lame story before he gets away. My heart is still trying to break through my rib cage when we drive back to the station. Before I can recollect my thoughts, a computer professor at Kentucky State University is online and offering to make the one-hour drive over here to perform a sex act on the boy.

This time, our station attorney gives me some advice: print out a transcript of the online conversation and use it to cross-examine the professor when he tries to talk his way out of this. Good idea. Watching the tape of my confrontation with Will reminds me of watching a high school football game tape on Monday, after I got blocked all over the field.

Same park. Same spot. Same actor. Completely different results. Marvin is bold enough to walk up with his K.S.U. sweatshirt on. Within one minute, he's boasting to our actor of his recent sexual exploits with a 14-year-old boy. "To Catch A Predator" will never be this good.

When we confront Marvin, he tries to convince us he drove over here as a computer professor to try to teach the boy he met online a lesson. He shouldn't be talking to men in chat rooms. It's dangerous.

"Because there are people out there like you," I reply. He insists he just came here to talk to the boy. So, I pull out the transcript and remind him he said things like, "I'll bend you over and show you how it's done."

There's no explaining statements like that. It's time to leave. He knows he's busted. But he has no idea how badly he's busted. Neither he, nor we, know that the FBI is parked out on the street and watching all of this. They are currently investigating the professor for sending child porn over the Internet. Before we can even get our investigation on the air, they slap the cuffs on Marvin and put him away for a long time. At his sentencing, he actually thanks us for showing him the error of his ways.

But the fact is, it doesn't matter how many reporters or cops do these undercover stings. Putting pedophiles on TV or sending them to prison appears to make no difference in the online predator problem.

In 1998, I do another online sting to show how predators get around the parental controls. In the same Louisville park, we confront and expose another pedophile trying to get to another 13-year-old boy. When the camera comes out, this guy loses it so badly, I honestly fear he's going to have a heart attack and die right there.

Ten years later, an undercover police sting in Louisville busts the same guy doing the same thing. No telling how many kids he got to over that decade of decadence.

MINI-MORTIFIED

Moments you can't plan for

It's one of the most popular half-marathons in the United States. The Kentucky Derby Festival Mini-Marathon is only half the distance of the full 26.2-mile marathon, but it's ballooning every year in participation. Well on its way to 15,000 runners, every possible aspect of the race has been covered. It's tough to scoop anyone. I've broadcast live via phone while running the race with the chopper right above me. I've interviewed a five months pregnant woman live while she was passing me at the six-mile mark. But today, I've found the ultimate 'mini' when it comes to the Mini-Marathon: a nine-year-old boy who is running this race for the fourth consecutive year.

Mind-blowing. He started running this testy 13.1 mile course when he was a kindergartner. I don't even think I'd let my kid start jogging around the block at the age of five. But this third grade race veteran has already worked his way up to a pace where he's just as fast as I am. I've interviewed Kenyans who can run this race at a pace of under five minutes per mile. I've interviewed someone who can run this race on a prosthetic leg. And I've interviewed guys who run this race dressed up like Elvis. But I'm most excited to do a live interview in our pre-race coverage with a third grader who has already run this race three times.

I can see he's nervous when his parents bring him over to me at my camera position near the start line. He has blonde hair and he reminds me of myself when I was nine, except for the part where he can run 13 miles.

He comes up only to my waist, so as soon as the anchors toss it to me, I turn and kneel down next to the boy, so I'm on his level. Kids usually make for tough interviews, but this one is exceptionally difficult. His answers are short and he gets more terrified as time goes by. His family members and the others surrounding us have this strange look on their faces, like they're witnessing a murder. It's not that bad, folks. I'm a professional. I'll get something good out of him.

After two minutes of bad TV, I look down and notice a huge puddle growing around the boy's running shoes. It hasn't rained in days, and nobody spilled anything to my knowledge. Then the stupid reporter understands why everyone's been horrified. The puddle is urine. The boy wet himself on live TV. I look back up and his panicked eyes are imploring me to get this microphone out of his face.

I abruptly end the interview and toss it back to the studio. The nine-year-old runner runs to the bathroom. I grab the camera and roll back the tape to see how this happened. Sure enough, the second I turned and knelt down next to him, the front of the boy's light gray shorts started turning dark. He reached down with his hands to try to cover the growing dark spot. He even clenched his legs together to try to stop the stream of urine dousing his shorts and flowing down to the pavement. Nothing worked. And the cruel, oblivious reporter kept firing questions at him until he noticed the puddle. A shell-shocked dad finally gets up the nerve to approach me with the $64,000 question.

"Do you think anyone at home noticed?"

Before I can lie my way out of this to try to make him feel better, my photographer chimes in.

"I think they probably did. The people back at the station could tell."

This is one of those times when a little lie would have been excusable and appropriate. The devastated dad shuffles off. Now the poor kid has to run thirteen miles in wet shorts and socks.

The crack of the gun is softer than I expected. The impact of the shot on the quivering puppy is more than I expected.

"When you kill the first dog, they know what's going on. They all just go inside there."

I can't look and neither can the other dogs. But he ropes them and drags them out individually anyway. He isn't as upset at what he's doing to the dogs as he is at what they are doing to him.

"I get blood on me a lot of times. It aggravates me that I have to get blood on my clothes, because I can't get it out."

I ask him about the American Veterinary Medical Association report that determined "gunshot should not be used for routine euthanasia in animal control situations."

His answer? "I don't know if it's as painful or not, because I ain't never been shot in the head."

Unable to argue with logic like that, and sick from what I am witnessing, I fumble ineptly through the rest of the shoot. Our shoot, I mean. We really don't know what we can put on TV, so we shoot the reaction of the other animals to each execution. They flinch and flee. After flinching too many times, it's time for me to flee. On the drive home, I ask my photographer to pull over, because I feel like I'm going to throw up.

We air the story and, surprisingly, not much happens. Then CNN picks it up, runs it every hour, and all hell breaks loose. While Kentucky viewers are unfazed by dog shooting, the rest of the world goes ballistic.

Wealthy animal rescuers fly in from San Francisco. The princess of a foreign country offers to fly all the unwanted dogs in Kentucky to safety in her homeland. Our station quickly puts together an animal rescue telethon that raises more than $40,000. Our annual telethon two weeks later for foster children in need of adoption raises only half that much. That's why I have a letter that says "Shoot the dog; save the children."

But as time passes in my life, it's becoming unmistakenly clear to me that people care far more about animals than they do about humans.

THE KILLING FIELDS

A slow death for gunshot euthanasia

D arrin stops shooting dogs. He is getting death threats. The chicken coop dog pound he pieced together at his relative's rural home is strafed in a drive-by shooting.

My stories hit the tabloids. After weeks of leading with the O.J. Simpson murder trial, "A Current Affair" leads one evening with a long piece they title, "Doggie Death Row." They use all my video, stir in some sensational language, and outrage even more people nationwide. But the rest of Kentucky keeps gunning down dogs. Lawmakers introduce legislation outlawing gunshot euthanasia. Truth is, marijuana has a better chance of being legalized here.

We continue doing dog-shooting stories all over Kentucky. In one county, the dog warden admits allowing jail inmates, on work release, to perform gunshot euthanasia. Somehow, handing a loaded gun to a convicted felon doesn't seem quite right to me, but I'm old school when it comes to prison rehab.

Then, in the middle of my daily dose of dozens of strange news tips, a soft-spoken man tells me he shot some video I have to see. He'd heard shots and shrieks out beyond the back of his farmland. He discovered a classic county animal shelter in Kentucky, hidden away on private property. Not

advertised, publicized or sanitized. Lost dogs have no chance
to be found or adopted here.

His video is worse than anything I've witnessed. Tiny
terriers and puny puppies dangle from the catchpole noose,
fighting so furiously, the shelter manager struggles to get a
shot placed squarely on the skull. Oftentimes, he misses the
mark, and the wounded dogs keep wriggling.

Most of the executions involve big dogs. Big dogs escape
home easier, but big dogs don't die easier. Many of them
have their legs locked, and feet dug in, as they are dragged
out to the killing field. Like the smaller dogs, they too often
require more than one shot, but not because they struggle.
Their brains are bigger. And a .22 caliber bullet is a far cry
from what Dirty Harry packed.

This video helps dispel the theory that a bullet to the brain
is the quickest, surest way of achieving instantaneous death.
These animals writhe in pain in between shots, convulsing
and howling so horribly that the middle-aged shooter has to
keep looking away. But when the cries die down, he tosses
them into the giant bucket of an endloader.

The image of dozens of dead or dying dogs, piled high
in the bucket, spilling out on the ground, tails still moving
in some cases, is enough to finally mobilize the masses.
Reforms get passed and politicians magically find more
money for animal shelters.

Ironically, that shelter manager had just completed
a euthanasia course and was fully certified in the
recommended euthanasia technique of lethal injection,
before unknowingly starring as the canine terminator.

PUBLIC SERVICE

Helping viewers the old-fashioned way

"Boel, run home and change into your shoveling gear," says my news director, "We're launching something new tonight."

Ah, yes, it's time for another one of those ideas that managers get paid to produce. I knew something was coming, because now we call ourselves "32 for You." We used to be "32 Alive," but our ratings are dead.

"32 for You" sounds good. Nice cadence. It rhymes. Rap is getting big. They're producing a "32 for You" song, too. Maybe they'll get Vanilla Ice to sing it. But for now, they're trying to come up with ways to make us the "For You" station. It snowed recently, so today I'm heading up the "32 for You Snow Patrol." The way it's explained to me, we're hooking up with local celebrities and shoveling out the driveways of the elderly and disabled. Just call in and we'll come dig you out.

Problem is, this isn't Mayberry. It's not just Floyd and Aunt Bee who need help. There are a lot of folks who need help in a TV market of almost a million people. I'm handed a shovel and a long list of homes to hit. But I'm not Santa Claus. I need help. They promise help is coming. And boy, am I relieved when I find out the University of Louisville football coach and members of his team are going to join me.

This might actually turn out to be cool. Me and a bunch of football players digging out snowbound old or disabled residents. At the first house, I do an interview with the sweet old lady, and then get to work. It's only four inches of snow, but it's a wet, heavy four inches. Nobody else shows up to help, so I knock it out in less than half an hour. I call back to the newsroom, asking where the football players are.

"Don't worry. They're on the way. Head to the next address. They'll meet you there."

The first thing I notice about the next home is it's a long, long way back from the street. I don't know if I can throw a football that far, much less shovel that long of a driveway. The elderly couple is so nice that I decide to start scooping. A half hour later, I'm halfway finished. Another call on my two-way radio back to the station. Another promise of assistance.

Another address, another solo shoveling gig. Two-a-day football practices in August weren't this grueling. Long after the driveways I've shoveled out-number the layers of sweaty clothing I've shed, it hits me like a ton of snow: I shoveled driveways to help pay for college, so I could come out and shovel driveways.

Then I get a call. The football team is not coming. Something got screwed up somewhere. Now they don't want me to do a live shot. They don't even want to run any video. The "32 for You Snow Patrol" isn't as interesting when John Boel is shoveling people out by himself. In fact, the "32 for You Snow Patrol" melts fast, and is never used again.

TAKE-HOME STORIES

TV news is stranger than fiction.

I t's hard to leave your work at work when you do this for a living. I come home to my own daughter every night with a picture in my head of another daughter. A two-year-old who weighs 13 pounds. Most of her fingernails and toenails have been removed. Her hair pulled out. At least seven major bones broken. Burns on her face, eyes and chest. Many of the burns are circles, suggesting she was a coaster for scalding cups of coffee.

Police in Southern Indiana call it the worst case of abuse they've ever seen. It's always the worst case of abuse they have ever seen. Until the next one. This is more than abuse. It's torture. The man accused of doing it told his best friend he was after insurance money to be paid if the child died of natural causes. The mom sat there and watched it all happen without trying to get help. They lived in a trailer down by the river.

Thirteen pounds at two years of age. My daughter is 13 pounds at the age of two months. I can't hold her close enough when I get home. It's impossible to be an unbiased journalist covering this story, or another one I'm following right now.

A guy named Ted Helfenbein decides to kill his little boy at a Memphis, Indiana, truck stop. He pulls over at 1:30 in the morning and shoots his son five times while he is sleeping in the back of his dad's Chevy Blazer. Then Ted drives to a pay phone to turn himself in. There is zero chance he will do an interview with me. When I get to the jail, he invites me in to set up the camera. I ask him how he pronounces his name and he says, "You know, Frankenstein, Einstein, Helfenbein."

He is closer to Frankenstein than Einstein. When told his boy still had a pulse after the shooting, he says, "I should have waited longer to call. Jesus, what does it take to kill him? I should have used the shotgun."

He tells me he shot his son fast, so he wouldn't feel any pain. Three in the head. Two in the chest. He says he did it because he didn't want his boy to suffer through the same life of poverty and hopelessness that he has endured. He calls it an act of love. I ask him why he didn't kill himself. He says suicide is a mortal sin and he doesn't want to go to hell.

I'll let God wrestle with that logic. I'm so gullible, I started to buy into his life-of-misery story. I need to get home to my daughter, because the third story I'm also following in Southern Indiana makes me want to ship her off to a private school far, far away.

A jealous sixteen-year-old lesbian and three other teenaged girls combine to pull off a crime that makes us freeze at our keyboards every time we have to write a new, grisly detail. Twelve-year-old Shanda Sharer is kidnapped, stripped, bound, beaten, throat-slashed, stabbed, strangled with rope and presumed dead. Each time she starts screaming or gurgling from the trunk, the car is stopped and she is stabbed some more or beaten with a tire iron. They spray Windex in her open wounds and marvel at the way the steam rises from them on a frosty January night. Unable to finish her off, they dump her in a field, douse her with gas, and set her on fire. They come back and torch her a second time for good measure, then drive straight to McDonald's where they have a big breakfast, rolling the burned sausage around on their plate and laughing about how it looks like Shanda.

I stare at the girls every day for weeks at their sentencing hearing. They don't look old enough to kill a fly. Cameras aren't allowed in Indiana courtrooms, so our video each day consists of the teens being ushered in and out of the building. Their friends and family members cuss us out. Kevin, my photographer, is attacked by a purse-flailing woman. We are vultures. We are cruel.

I may be. But I haven't touched McDonald's breakfast sausage since.

DYING TO LEAVE

More pain around us than we like to admit

Another thought-provoking church sermon. The message: God never gives us more than we can handle. My mind is still swimming around the topic when I walk over to a room where I volunteer to assist people who want help in prayer.

With tears rolling down their faces, a couple wants to pray for a relative. They explain how he was going through a divorce. The source of his pain was the guilt of leaving his five-year-old daughter. When his weekend with her was over and it was time to leave the home where he used to live, he tucked her in, kissed her forehead, then went back to his apartment and killed himself.

I'm not much help to them because of a horrible flashback. I went through the very same thing years earlier in my life when my wife and I were split. The pain and guilt I suffered each time I handed over my five-year-old daughter was almost unbearable. I vividly remember lying all night on the floor of my apartment, sobbing, even wailing in grief, unable to even get up and get in bed.

My mind wanders back to the sermon topic. God never

gives us more than we can handle. I start calling up several horrible examples, just from my own family, where loved ones with more than they could handle have committed suicide.

My brother-in-law, struggling with alcoholism, shot himself after three failed rehab attempts.

My cousin, at the age of 14, shot himself in the yard behind his house.

His dad, my uncle, got under the car in his garage and gassed himself to death out of the grief less than a month after his son's death.

The most troubling, unexplainable events of my life involve suicides. I still wonder why my young cousin felt compelled to shoot himself. I still remember the smell of the flowers at his funeral right before Christmas. And when I remember how close I was to doing the same thing, I realize how thin the line is between happiness and deadly despair.

It may be the most complex, important story subject out there. But when a death turns out to be a suicide, the media almost always dismisses it. I understand the reasons why, but there is so much I don't understand about suicide.

And it happens so often, it makes me want to report the stories behind every one of them, in caring detail, so the rest of us can learn something from it. I'm still having a hard time with the notion that God never gives us more than we can handle, because many of the victims of suicide were incredible Christians who appeared to be enjoying an enviable walk with God.

BIG BLUE MADNESS

Get your priorities straight.

People always struggle to try to convey how big University of Kentucky basketball is in the Bluegrass. They use words like "religion." They drop bad clichés all the time. The fact is, it's really bigger than any word can quantify. For the 15th time in a 16-year span, Kentucky led the nation in home basketball game attendance. But it's bigger than any statistic. It skews priorities so badly, other people would refuse to believe it. Packers fans in Green Bay would laugh. Red Sox fans in Boston would bristle. But I can sum it all up in one, true story.

On February 27, 1994, much of America is glued to the gold medal hockey game in Lillehammer, the curtain-closing event of the XVII Winter Games. It is one of the longest hockey games in Olympic history, and many call it the most dramatic. That's right, more dramatic than that "miracle on ice" thing in 1980.

Canada has not won the hockey gold medal in more than four decades. Sweden has never won it. After desperate, violent, end-to-end rushes, Canada scores twice in three minutes, then Sweden ties it at 2, with less than two minutes remaining. They cannot settle it in 60 minutes of regulation. The tense 10-minute overtime is fiercely fought, but no one scores. Now we go to what many people wish hockey and soccer would just do anyway: the heart-stopping shootout. Five players from each team take turns firing shots at the other team's goalie, one-on-one. Few things in sports are this intense.

The shooters take turns, and they tie again. So for the first time in Olympic history, the gold medal game goes to sudden death. Each team gets one shot. It only continues if they both tie again.

Sweden's Magnus Svensson loosens up, then takes off toward the puck . . . and the goal . . . and then . . .

Bam. Time for the Rick Pitino show.

WKYT-TV, the flagship station of Kentucky Wildcat basketball, rolls the Rick Pitino show instead. Hey, the Cats play at 1 P.M. with the coach's show as a preview before tip-off.

The general manager later apologizes. "We made a mistake," says Ralph Gabbard. "It was a bad decision. We can't take it back. A department head made the decision she thought was right. She didn't understand the seriousness of going for the gold."

One Lexington resident calls it, "the greatest error in judgment since the infamous Heidi game." In that one, NBC rolled the TV movie *Heidi* when there were 65 seconds left of a game that had the Jets leading the Oakland Raiders by 3. Those viewers missed seeing two more touchdowns scored.

In the gold medal hockey game sudden death shootout, Kentucky viewers miss Peter Forsberg's legendary hesitation move that freezes the goalie and wins it for the Swedes, 3 to 2.

But more importantly, UK crushes Georgia 80 to 59 after the Rick Pitino show. And, most importantly, only 20 people call WKYT to complain about the sudden death switch.

In Kentucky, sudden death happens if you don't run the coach's show and the Cats game on time.

A REAL CHARACTER

Reasons to savor life are all around us.

Sometimes in this business, we miss the best stories. Compelling characters are right there in front of us, and we don't realize it.

I meet him during my involvement with Team in Training, a charity that raises money for cancer research. I have no idea he has nearly died from cancer many times. After spending time with him, I am sure he will never die from cancer.

We're training for a triathlon to be held at Walt Disney World. In the pool, I notice the scars all over his back and chest and stomach, but I haven't put it together. He always cracks jokes and he's constantly high on life. David Schneider has the melanoma carved out of him. In its place, the doctors must have implanted seeds of joy.

At Team in Training practice sessions, I focus on following my coaches, improving my swim stroke, and becoming a better biker. David is focused on laughing, listening, and lapping up every ounce of the mundane details left in the day's dog dish.

I file stories about every facet of Team in Training. The

$75,000 raised by our group for leukemia research. The little girl receiving a bone marrow transplant in two weeks. The motivational experts crossing the country teaching ordinary people how to raise big bucks for great causes.

But David is a regular. Not a regular recipient of these cancer donations during his wicked battle. He is a regular fundraiser for Team in Training. His friends even pitch in their own money to buy him a new triathlon bike after one of his surgeries. But he doesn't need a glistening new bike to motivate him to get back out there as soon as he can stumble out of bed.

I'm not as friendly to him as I should be, but he calls me from time-to-time to go to lunch or just shoot the bull. Often, when the phone rings, I'm busy and I brush him off.

Years later, we're having a great time at a Christmas ball. The band is loud. The liquor is flowing. The dresses are delectable. At the happiest moment of the night, he whispers something in my ear.

"Tumor's back."

I freeze. Not at the news as much as the timing. The moment. How can that happen? He goes on to explain that a couple of spots have popped up on his latest scan. He doesn't try to spin the bad news very much. I can't concentrate the rest of the night, but David appears to be having the time of his life.

He keeps calling. I keep trying to make him laugh. He loves hearing TV news stories. I never take the initiative to call him first.

When we finally meet for lunch again, I am horrified. If I didn't know he was coming, I wouldn't recognize him. He is thin and gaunt and carved up from surgeries. He looks like one of those Auschwitz survivors in the Holocaust. But he says this is the best he's looked and felt in months. He's been driving himself all the way to West Virginia and back, once a week, to receive experimental treatments. His cancer is exploding inside. But he feels like the luckiest man alive, because he talked one hospital into a life-saving surgery that no one else would attempt, and he says he would be dead by now if they had not consented to try.

We talk about running and biking together again soon, but I can't imagine that will ever happen. I'm so shocked at how cancer has ravaged his body, I can't eat. He can't either.

I leave the sandwich shop feeling proud of myself, because I made him laugh a lot. Humor is what he needs. He walks away with a smile, ready to devour the rest of the day, because there aren't many left.

When I get home, I pop a pill for depression, and realize what a joke I am for doing so.

the viewing area before the snowstorm began. By planning ahead, Goliath crushed David in its coverage content. But more importantly, Goliath stayed on the air for 30 more minutes than David. So Goliath again pounded his chest as the best. The ramifications were felt for years in the Louisville television war.

"This will never happen again," bellowed my boss. And he was right. The snow coverage arms race snowballed.

As the earth moved closer to the turn of the century, weather forecasting gadgetry got more sophisticated. Man could now also see what God saw coming, or so he thought. TV stations could now lead every newscast for three days with a three-inch snowfall forecast. And the people became afraid. They heard "snow is coming" on every station, leading every newscast, for days. They panicked, dashing to the store for milk and bread. TV stations did live reports from the grocery stores on the shelf-emptying panic that erupted from their own forecasts. Viewers saw this and jumped in their cars to join them. And the supermarket owners saw that this was good. Feeding off its own fear, the abominable snow monster grew exponentially. When the pretty three-inch snowfall finally arrived, people had forgotten there was very little at stake.

By 2004 AD, a great fleet of state and local snow removal equipment was assembled. The Louisville area had gathered more snowplows per mile of roadway than many cities to the north that receive much more snow. Idling at interstate interchanges for hours, they waited to pounce on the first flakes. The mayor, long ago lambasted for snow removal response, saw that it was good. One member of his staff was appointed to repeat, "The city is prepared," to every TV station every time they needed to fill extended coverage time.

School systems that once took pride in refusing to call off classes based on forecasts began shutting down long before a flake flew. When just under 100,000 students in Louisville were sent home at lunchtime on a fear-filled day and it never snowed, an anchor named John, whom Jesus loved, posed tough questions to the school official who made the decision. He was not pleased. Many viewers were also not pleased with John, though there was more dandruff on his suit coat than snow on the sidewalk. After all, 'tis better to be safe than sorry when it comes to snow, or the possibility of snow. Through January 10 of 2009, the official weather service total snowfall amount for the entire winter was 1.3 inches. Yet several school systems had already called off school several times.

Cold weather during winter was feared as well. On January 15, dozens of school systems delayed classes because the temperature was five degrees above zero outside. A two-hour delay was just as chaotic on many working parents as an outright cancellation, but one school official explained to the "armchair quarterbacks" that it prevented students from standing out in the dark at that time of the morning in such cold weather. He did not mention that it's always dark at that time of the morning in January, and the temperature after the two-hour delay was measured at one degree warmer.

Elsewhere in the news that day: an Alaska school district

that had never cancelled school before, refused to call off classes again despite that day's temperature of 60 below zero. And the daily tour of Lambeau Field in Green Bay, Wisconsin, was sold out, despite an air temperature of 22 below zero.

But winter weather fear spread to even the most rugged northern cities. By 2010 AD, the Philadelphia Eagles broke new ground by postponing their home pro football game because of a 12-inch snow forecast. Pennsylvania's governor was outraged.

"We cancel the game and there's less than three inches of snow. We've become a nation of wusses."

Back in Louisville, in-car cameras beamed live pictures to viewers that show the rest of the world getting to where they need to go in the snow. One terrified e-mailer said she couldn't get out of her house because her road was impassable. Another e-mailer said he just drove that road and it was fine. The number of hours of extended live TV coverage of snow is now often greater than the number of inches of snow on the ground.

The TV executives saw that it was good, because the people kept watching.

COCKY FIGHTERS

To question them is un-American.

J oin a cockfighting club and get $500 off your next Toyota car or truck.

Sound like a bad redneck joke? Nope. It's true, and only in Kentucky.

When I take a call, claiming the largest Toyota truck center in the Midwest is helping to fund a group with a history of involvement in organizing illegal criminal cockfighting in Kentucky, I have my doubts. But there it is, a full-page magazine ad, boasting a financial incentive for auto buyers who are members of the Kentucky United Gamefowl Breeders Association. Members get a $500 discount on a car or truck purchase, and the Toyota dealer in Lexington donates $100 to the group for each vehicle sold.

You see, one thing you can't call Kentucky cockfighters is "chicken."

The Kentucky Derby happens once a year. Kentucky cockfighting derbies happen once a month, at huge, well-known arenas. Even though they're illegal, they advertise the events, too. So, we take a little hidden camera trip down to one of them in Williamsburg.

This event is held at a place creatively and appropriately named Roost Arena. It isn't hard to find. There are signs out on the highways directing people to Roost Arena. Clearly, police are well aware of what's going on.

We walk in and find hundreds of people in stadium seating. The padded, fold-down chairs are nicer than what we use in Louisville theaters. The entry fee is ten dollars for humans, but 150 bucks for birds. The chicken gets to fight for his life. If he survives, the trainer gets a trophy.

I notice 47 gamecocks are entered. They start fighting in the caged-in "main" pit, which is cockfighting's version of Wimbledon's Center Court. If a quick death doesn't occur, the birds are dragged off into one of the many "drag" pits all around Roost Arena, where they gouge and slash each other for up to an hour. One of the handlers is wearing a shirt, displaying bloody chickens, that reads, "Till death do us part."

In a weird way, it's like watching gladiators in a coliseum, fighting to the death. In a humorous way, it's like watching traders on the floor of the New York Stock Exchange. But these traders are wearing bib overalls, screaming over the hundreds of dollars they've invested in wagers. In a very real way, it's like watching sauced football fans, with roars of cheers and boos rising up out of these poultry playoffs.

Of course, in this sport, they sharpen long metal gaffs or knives and attach them to the birds' legs. I'm no prude. I used to hunt. But I'd have to rate this performance "PG"-Pretty Gory.

Still, I notice flocks of children all around Roost Arena.

There's blood all over the place, and people step over the losing birds on their way out. I don't have much of an appetite, but I notice a cafeteria in Roost Arena, with a big menu, including hot dogs, hamburgers, fries and pizza.

One thing not on the menu: chicken. Not even wings.

VIEWER FEEDBACK

Nothing is sacred when their program is interrupted.

H ang up the phone, and it rings again. Five seconds don't pass before another call rolls over to me. "Adopt-a-thon, may I help you?"

It's two weeks before Christmas. In our annual one-hour prime time special, we are taking pledges and providing adoption information for the Wednesday's Child program. For 25 years, our station has been airing weekly profiles of foster children who need to be adopted. They've been removed from their homes due to neglect or abuse, and their stories are often too heartbreaking to detail on air. It doesn't matter. The moment they speak, or even look at the camera, it's enough to make you cry. Osama bin Laden would have called in and pledged a donation for these poor kids. In the middle of a fast and furious night of record-setting donations, I take a stunning call.

"Adopt-a-thon, how may I help you?"

"When are you going to get this crap off the air?"

"Excuse me?"

"I'm sitting here waiting for my show to come on, and you're running this garbage instead."

Still unable to comprehend what is happening, I explain this is the Wednesday's Child Adopt-a-thon, and we are taking financial donations, as well as inquiries, for children who don't have a permanent home.

"I look forward all week to my show, and I come home from work, and you put this bull---- on. Nobody cares about this."

Finally, it sets in. This is no joke. This is a joke of a human being who is outraged that we moved his show to a different time slot. Instead of getting his name and address and personally driving over and beating him bloody, I decide to appeal to his humanity.

"But sir, it's Christmas time, and we're trying to help hundreds of kids who've been taken away from their abusive parents, placed in foster care or group homes and, in many cases, have gone years without any kind of family to call their own."

"So then why don't you put this special kids crap on on the weekend, when nobody's watching anyway, like the other station does with their Crusade for Children?"

"Sir, do you have any kind of heart at all? I mean, I can't believe I'm having this conversation with you."

"And I can't believe you ----ers would put this ---- on TV tonight."

At this point, I hang up. Jesus Himself would give up, too. Besides, this guy has already cost the kids a couple hundred dollars in missed donations just in the time he's taken up. But he is far from unusual when it comes to how low people can go when their programs get interrupted.

When the space shuttle blows up for the second time, our station has a decision to make. We're scheduled to air a college basketball game, but the network news operations insist on covering this trivial astronaut disaster. The game between the University of Louisville and Indiana University has been scheduled as the nationally televised CBS game, and with Louisville being on the Indiana border, it's an especially important game for local basketball fans here.

But when CBS decides a space shuttle disaster trumps a college basketball game, it's a bad time to be in our newsroom. Tip-off, or blast-off gone horribly wrong? The calls start pouring in.

"Where's the game?"

"The space shuttle has exploded," I answer. "Everyone's dead. It's kind of a huge story."

"What's wrong with you idiots," the next caller screams. "Why ain't the Louisville game on?"

And it only gets worse. The profanity picks up. The call volume climbs. Soon, we can't keep up with the angry avalanche.

"It's about time that f---ing thing blew up," one caller yells. "That damn shuttle's been sucking the government dry for years."

I hang up the phone and walk out the door, shaking my head.

Then I listen to the basketball game all the way home on my radio.

OUT IN THE COLD

Walking in their shoes for as long as I can

When summer arrives, newscasts often contain stories on the heat. When winter blows in, you constantly see stories on the cold. There is nothing unusual about cold in the winter or heat in the summer unless something newsworthy happens because of it. But you'd never know that by watching local and even national news.

So, oftentimes you see a reporter standing out in the heat, doing a story on how outdoor workers have to drink a lot of water. Most of the time, workers out in the heat sweat a lot, too. It's fascinating.

Or you get a reporter out in the cold, bundled up in a heavy, expensive coat, telling us how the homeless shelters are full, and there are still homeless people who refuse to come inside. But we never actually see those poor folks.

Do they really exist? Are there people in Louisville, Kentucky, who refuse to come inside even when the temperature drops to the single digits in January and February? After years of watching this ritual from the anchor desk, I doubt it, but I'm going to get some answers.

I have a great idea. I'm going to go out and find them, live with them, and tell their survival story. Or I'm going to debunk an urban legend.

When I call my friends at the biggest homeless shelter in town, they agree to introduce me to such an encampment. But they say it's going to be tough to talk them into the story. I refuse to believe it. But after a few trips to meet and talk with them, I learn my friends weren't kidding. Homeless people don't like TV news stories on homeless people. They don't like cameras and they especially don't like reporters giving away their secret living locations, because cops roll in and chase them out.

But somehow, after repeated negotiations and clothing donations, I talk one group into it. I manage to talk Scott, my photographer, into trying this with me. He's worried. I'm not.

I'm a tough guy. I go ice fishing. I've fallen through the ice three times and continued fishing for several more hours with frozen clothes. I wear shorts year-round here. So with a forecast low of 14 degrees and some sleet, this is going to be a piece of cake when we're all bundled up.

The homeless guy who is going to put us up for the night says he used to work in a homeless shelter. He's not your stereotypical homeless guy. He's not alcoholic, not crazy and not a criminal. He's just an old man who got tired of life, tired of people telling him what to do, and set out on his own. He sets us up in a gutted shell of an old school bus. Tarps are strung up over the smashed out windows to block the wind. This looks warmer than the ice fishing shanties we use in Wisconsin.

The other guys who live here have a wood-burning stove built into the side of their school bus shell. Talk about a fire trap. No smoke alarms. They're more concerned with survival than safety.

This group reinforces the classic homeless stereotypes. The alcoholics and mentally ill middle-aged men sit around drinking ultra-cheap beer and remembering their buddies who've frozen to death. Every once in a while we read stories on the news about hypothermia deaths in the winter, but I didn't realize so many of them were homeless.

They take us on a walk to introduce us to other homeless encampments. Most of these people live in ice-encased bubble tents. I'm struck by how close they are to office buildings and businesses with dozens of windows that look out on them. They're right in our midst, yet we don't see them. Or we look past them on purpose.

They're warming up to me. But I'm getting cold. There's no car to get in to warm up for a minute. There's no heated bathroom around. In fact, there's no bathroom around.

And when it's finally time to go to bed, there is no bed. Think about that. These people haven't used even a bad bed for years. My sleeping bag on the floor of the bus is a joke. Sleet pellets are somehow finding their way past the tarp curtains and they're pinging off my frozen face.

Come to think of it, I've never spent the night on the floor of an ice-fishing shanty. And we always had one of those sweet Coleman heaters kicking out warmth.

Scott keeps changing positions every 15 minutes. He's trying to find a fetal position that maximizes self-warming.

Every time I come close to actual sleep, a roar of laughter or yelling from the drunken guys in one of the other buses wakes me up. They've got the secret. They drink until they pass out.

At 3:45 A.M., I turn to Scott.

"Had enough?"

"Yes," he barks back.

My lips no longer work. But that's okay. There's no need for further conversation. Two yellow-bellied journalists creep back to their stashed car and head for a warm bed. We didn't even make it through one night.

RACISM

Challenging the protest machine brings it to our front door.

My special report is scheduled to air in 20 minutes, but already protestors are arriving outside the TV station. Dozens of them are outside the front door. The same protestors we videotape at every protest in town. They're here to protest a story they haven't seen yet, because it hasn't aired.

They assume it's going to be racist and biased. They're chanting "W-K-K-K." The station manager is not here and no one knows what to do. I offer to go out and speak to them, but I'm denied. I want to ask them why they're protesting something they haven't even seen yet.

Actually, that's not as ridiculous as it sounds. Ninety percent of the people who call or e-mail me to complain about a story I did never actually viewed the story. They heard or assumed something, or based their complaint on the promo they saw before the newscast.

They're holding professionally printed red and white signs that read, "Money is no subsitute for equality." The first thing we notice is there's no substitute for proper spelling. They omitted that first "t." All of their signs are misspelled. It's not the first time.

It's my guess they're here protesting a story they haven't seen because they know exactly what's been going on. The investigation looks deeper into the actions of the leading civil rights activist in town. Basically, he calls in the TV cameras and stages protests until the allegedly racist company or government agency awards his group a "minority hiring" contract. When I examine how much work he then does to earn the money, and his results, the answer is not much. Or "nothing" as one city official puts it. If you question what's going on, as one commissioner did, you're called a "racist."

Some call it hush money. Some call it extortion. I call it fascinating, because he's using the media to get what he wants, and we follow along every time. The legal meetings got ugly at times, but credit my managers for having the guts to air a controversial story that shows every news operation in Louisville as unknowing participants in an alleged extortion scheme.

This time, their protest is going to get them no money. We air a live shot of their protest on our property at the end of the first report. As soon as they've gotten on TV, they scatter, leaving their misspelled signs littering the front lawn.

A week later one of the high-profile leaders of the protest walks into the sandwich shop where I'm eating lunch She was the one who started the "W-K-K-K" chant.

Oh, no. Here it comes.

She sits down at the table right next to me. But she does not berate me. In fact, she smiles and starts asking me questions about the TV business these days. Clearly, she still hasn't seen the story, and has no idea I'm the one who did it.

I still have one of her misspelled signs in my garage.

PUBLIC PARK PLEASURE

Reality TV at the best pick-up place in town

The sweat pours off me like a faucet turned wide open. I'm sitting on a picnic table overlooking the Ohio River at a public park in Louisville. Nice breeze. Beautiful view.

Only one problem: men keep walking up and asking me if I want to have sex. No foreplay. No discretion. They don't even ask my first name. The hidden camera and microphone under my shirt capture everything.

"Ever thought about being with another man before?" the first visitor asks.

"Hi," I reply.

Where I'm from, you at least say hello before propositioning someone for sex. But not here. This is Eva Bandman Park, one of many public parks advertised on the Internet as a great place for men to meet and have sex. I was sent here to see if an ordinary citizen, sitting in a public park, is subjected to lewd or perverted activity.

The practice isn't new, but the TV coverage of it is. It began at a Texas TV station. At the end of a jaw-dropping special report that even showed the male sex acts going on, the horrified news anchor apologized to the viewers, basically saying in its lust for ratings points, the station had lost its sense of decency in allowing that report to air.

He got in big trouble. The report was then replicated in almost every local news market in the United States. The guy assigned to it in Louisville for the first time: John Boel.

"I'll give you a b--- --- if you got a place to do it," one guy offers. He stands right there in front of me and starts masturbating. Man, if he only knew the hidden camera under my shirt is capturing all of this, and he's going to be a porn star on the evening news. I get up and walk to another spot in the park. He follows me and picks back up where he left off. I move again, and he follows again.

This guy is driving a marked van, with the name of a very well-known plumbing contractor on his vehicle and on his shirt. As he tinkers with his own plumbing, I want to show him my hidden camera. But instead, I flee to our surveillance van.

"You're lousy at this," my photographer laughs.

"Then, let's switch," I fire back, sweat pouring off my nose. "I'll stay here and shoot this and you go out there."

"No way, man," he says. So I call it a day.

But I have to come up with something, so I head back out. This time I pull in and park at Cox Park on the Ohio River. The camera I have taped to the passenger side door captures something my colleagues can't believe. A mere eight seconds after I shift the car into park, a middle-aged man pulls in next to me. He immediately gets out, walks over to my window, and while manipulating his manhood, asks me a question.

"Want a b--- ---?"

Again, not even a hello first.

"No, thanks," I reply, realizing I won't even have to edit the tape this time to show how fast you get solicited for sex in these parks.

The ratings for these reports are higher than for anything I've ever done. So, I am sent out to do more. I interview a Louisville cop who says he made 70 sodomy arrests in one park, in one summer, for this stuff. And that was 28 years ago. He arrested other police officers, funeral home directors, teachers, car salesmen but, fortunately, no TV reporters.

I interview another officer who recently made 117 public park pervert arrests, including nine ministers and eight teachers. Most fascinating are the demographics of this. He crunched the arrest numbers and found the average park pervert who gets caught is a 51-year-old white, married male. I go out with him on one of his undercover missions and witness something that trumps everything I have already observed.

While we videotape another in a series of white, married, fifty-something-year-old males being handcuffed and hauled away in an Indiana park, we notice an old man just sitting in his car, watching it all. After deciding we have more than enough material, and realizing this is like shooting fish in a barrel, we decide to leave. Our marked news car, and the marked police cars, all stream past the guy who's been watching. He then promptly drives over to our undercover officer, sticks his arm out of his open car window, and begins massaging the officer's groin area. Clearly the dumbest or horniest man on earth, he is hauled in to the nearby police post.

This is an interview I have to do. We walk over, fire up the camera, extend the microphone and start asking questions.

"You were watching the officers bust men for the very same thing. Then you did it, too. What were you thinking?"

He mumbles something, and then I notice a stain soaking his pants. The dirty old man just defecated in his drawers.

We pack up our gear and drive furiously to get back to the station. We want to laugh until we cry, but we can't. We're too sick. Finally, my photographer says, "Boel, you finally did it. You finally scared the crap out of someone."

IN THE NAME OF GOD

Is God really to blame for all of this?

It happens almost daily. Sometimes it happens several times in the same newscast. People love to explain tragedy and triumph by throwing everything in God's lap. I have serious problems with it in many ways.

On Christmas Eve, we report the story of an 11-year-old Amish girl who ran out to give the mail carrier some Christmas candy, and a passing driver who didn't see her mowed her down dead.

Two minutes later, in the same newscast segment, we tell the amazing survival story of a woman who was buried for three days underneath 23 inches of snow. In her case, a relative concluded, "I think God literally reached down and cradled her until we could find her."

In the case of the 11-year-old Amish girl, her relative told us, "It wasn't the driver's fault. It was just God's way of taking her out of this world."

I believe in a higher power. I'm pretty cool with the Christian Bible's version of God. But is He really pulling the strings on things like this? I grasp the concept that no matter how bizarre it may seem to us, God can intervene in our lives and take us out or save us for reasons we can't grasp at the time. But does he really decide to "call home" an 11-year-old girl out trying to promote the Christmas spirit, but then decide to save a woman buried for days in the snow despite her own incompetence?

Right before those two stories came the story of a 23-year-old Xavier University graduate student, devoted to God and a lifelong example of what we should all strive to be. She's in a Christmas play at her mega-church, with 2500 men, women and children watching. Hanging from a cable, playing one of the wise men in the nativity story, she plummets 25 feet to her death right in the middle of the audience.

I read the girl's bio. Purely, an angel. To all the people who say, "God decided this was the time to call her home," I say, there's no way.

This is a nativity story, at Christmas time, trying to attract people to the wonderful story of Jesus. So God's going to pull the string and show doubters and children a horrible death of someone trying to promote the message?

And then comes the ice storm of 2009. The worst power outage in Kentucky history. More than 600,000 homes left in the dark for days at the coldest time of the year. Two dozen deaths and counting. One of them, a 74-year-old woman in Radcliff, who went to bed in a trailer with no power or heat and never woke up. She froze to death.

"It was freezing cold," her 62-year-old husband said. "I reached over to touch my wife, and she was ice cold. I guess when God says it's time, that's it."

Maybe. Or maybe the heart and kidney problems the coroner said she suffered from made her more susceptible to freezing to death in a sub-freezing trailer without heat for two days.

The next time you hear people on the news chalk up a miracle, or a miserable tragedy, to the sprawling puppet show they believe God is manipulating at every moment, you might want to at least question what God's involvement really was. When I get my one-on-one interview with Him, it's going to be my first question.

SECURITY BREACH

A slow news day meets a slow terrorist-hunting day.

What's that phrase? ". . . like trying to break into Fort Knox . . ." Apparently, that's what they think I'm trying to do.

My boss wants me to do a special report on the mysterious gold vault at Fort Knox. It's in our viewing area and very little has been known about it since it was built in 1933. Since the 9/11 terrorist attack, the United States Bullion Depository is reportedly high on the terrorists' hit list because of its symbolic value to the United States. Of course, that's according to some unnamed source somewhere. Al Qaida hasn't actually divulged that list. In the post 9/11 world, you can claim pretty much anything and it's accepted as true if it threatens Americans.

If there is such a thing as "mission impossible" in journalism, this assignment may be it. Is there really gold stored in the Bullion Depository? How much? Some say there's anywhere from 200 to 900 billion dollars worth of gold stored there. Others claim the place is protected by minefields, ground-sweeping radar, and laser beam-triggered machine guns. Of course, I can't get anybody with any authority to confirm or deny any of this. And I can't get any video of the inside of the vault. In its history, there has only been one staged tour of the depository for politicians and media. They allowed only one TV cameraman inside for the 1974 tour. Fortunately, the pool photographer was from my station. Unfortunately, we cannot find the film he shot.

It appears the only thing I know I can get for this report is a picture of the outside of the place. After all, thousands of people drive right by it every day on a busy roadway. A public roadway. And the Fort Knox website clearly allows photos of the gold vault from the street outside. So when we pull over on Dixie Highway and start shooting video of the same building thousands of people see every day, no one seems to care. Then my photographer asks me a question.

"Check this out. What are all those guys doing, dressed up like Spiderman?"

Sure enough, a half-mile away, figures in skin-tight black clothing, head-to-toe, are emerging through holes in the roof of the gold depository. They look like fleeing insects. They really are dressed like Spiderman. They're fanning out and apparently coming to get us.

"Should we go?" he asks.

"Why? We're not doing anything wrong."

Long before the spidermen can scurry over to us half a mile away, we're surrounded by MPs, "Mint Police." They fly up in vehicles with flashing lights. They run up onto the elevated roadway from the fields and yards below. They're out of breath, out of practice and out of patience.

"What are you doing?" asks the first huffing and puffing Mint Police officer.

"We're taking pictures of the outside of the gold depository for a feature story we're working on."

"You can't do that."

"What do you mean I can't do that? I'm standing on a public roadway, not private property. We're taking pictures of the same thing anyone can take a picture of from any of the cars that pass by here every day. And as of this morning, your website allows photographs of the outside of the building from off the property."

None of that matters to him. He treats us like we're terrorists. We don't look like Al-Qaida. A white man sweating in a suit, riding in a brightly marked local news vehicle, isn't much of a threat.

"I need you to give me your videotape," he insists.

I've never been one of those big First Amendment crusaders, but this is just plain wrong.

"No, I'm not going to do that. I'm well within my rights as a journalist and I'm not doing anything wrong. I'm taking pictures of something 10,000 people drive by every day."

We show him the video we've recorded already to convince him we're not an Al-Qaida security breach.

"I'm sorry. I'm going to have to insist you give me your tape."

Wow. For twenty years, I've read about these kinds of First Amendment standoffs. But they involve information that can solve murder cases or catch criminals. I never thought it would happen to me, especially in a situation like this. But I'm in a big one now.

"What happens if I don't surrender my tape?"

"Then you'll have to be detained."

"I'm being detained right now. You mean I'll go to jail?"

"Yes. Just give me the tape and you can be on your way."

This is definitely not the kind of story I would have selected to take my first big First Amendment stand of defiance, but this is outrageous. This is the United States of America, not Iraq. With fingers shaking in anger, I call my news director, as well as our station's attorney. I'm willing to go to jail over this one. But they instruct me to turn over the videotape. Their reasoning makes no sense to me, but it will after I cool down.

9/11 is still too painful to the public. Everything the government does is justified. Reporters like me are un-American if we don't play along. When people read that a reporter has been jailed for trying to take pictures of the gold vault, they won't even get to the facts before they pass judgment that I was in the wrong. I can't win.

Handing over the tape makes me sick to my stomach. The Mint Police head back to the vault, victorious in what is probably their most exciting confrontation of the year.

A couple of nights later, our chopper gets plenty of great aerial pictures of the gold vault property while shooting the Friday night high school football game right next door. Good thing Al-Qaida isn't watching.

WHITE BOY IN THE HOOD

No hope, lots of dope, and a dope hiding in a van

I'm supposed to be afraid, but I'm appalled. I should be scared, but I'm sad. I'm surrounded by danger, but I'm consumed by depression.

Parked on the most dangerous corner in Louisville, I'm hunkered down in the back of a surveillance van. More sweat is pouring down my body than during any triathlon I've tried. The dark clothing I'm wearing matches the dark carpet and seats around me. If you looked right at me through the black tinted window, you probably wouldn't see the nervous white journalist clutching the camera.

No boss would ever assign someone to this story. Too much liability. I assigned myself. This place pops up way too often in the crime stories I read on the news. Passing cop cars riddled with bullets. People pulled out of vehicles and murdered in front of everybody.

My latest investigative project is in a housing project. I'm trying to capture drug dealing on tape. Everyone says drugs are behind the staggering crime rate here. They blame the cops for not doing enough. On my first day, with police cars all over the place, I almost turned around and left. No chance to videotape drug dealing with cops walking around and driving by every couple of minutes.

Fortunately, I was wrong. The most popular economic stimulus package in this neighborhood is a white rock in a plastic baggie. Point a camera in any direction and somebody's dealing drugs. I'm rolling on drug deals even when I don't realize it. I get back to the station and slow down or zoom in on things and sure enough, they're passing cash and crack.

They even stash the stuff in their mouths, like squirrels, and deal directly from there in case a customer is a cop and they have to swallow it. They stand out in the street like airport runway workers and direct customers into a crack drive-thru lane that's more efficient than any fast food place.

The stats show 90 percent of the crimes committed here are by people who don't live here. Sure enough, I videotape carloads of people who roll up, get out and start working the neighborhood as door-to-door crack salesmen. But as the hours and days go by, something else is emerging that's more impactful to me than anything I'm capturing on camera.

Whether you're a detective or a journalist, surveillance is fascinating. You're planted in a time and space where you're invisible. You get to know the daily routines of everything around you, from the moment when the sun peeks through each day, to the arrival times of parents and school buses.

Watching life go by in a housing project is the most dismal reality show I've ever witnessed. It appears that nobody's working. Few are in school. At 11 A.M. on a school day, clusters of middle and early high school-aged boys are right out there dealing drugs. Their younger brothers and sisters are watching, or training for the jobs. Responsible fathers are rare. Moms the age of my college sophomore daughter are herding up their children and trying to navigate life. When a teenaged dad does bother to go over and pick up his kid, nobody but me knows his pockets are loaded with crack rocks. Then again, maybe everybody knows. But I'm the only one videotaping it.

Huge crowds of people are standing outside, round the clock, even on brutally cold January days. I understand why, as my mind wanders back to the many times I've been in these tiny, filthy housing project apartments with cement block walls. It's a lot like prison. Clearly, these people can't wait to get out of their prison cells. Problem is, what they're doing outside is going to get them sent to prison. Or put in a casket.

I'm here because of the danger. But I'm depressed because of the future. These kids are doomed. The three Rs will be replaced by the three Ds: dropping out, dealing drugs and doing time. If they're lucky, they'll just be unemployed.

After my reports air, my house gets covered by graffiti. My wife and daughter are sobbing. Somebody found where I live and spray-painted death threats all over the garage. My bosses decide to hire police to guard my house and family for the next 72 hours.

But I'm not scared. Not one bit. And it's not because I'm a tough guy. As I gaze out the window at round-the-clock police presence on the street in front of my East End house, in my East End life, all I can think of is those poor kids in the housing project. They're the ones who need protection. They're doomed. And nobody's doing anything about it.

TROY STORY

Made-for-TV weight loss battles have sad endings too.

Troy Jackson died today. I knew that was going to happen. He knew death was a distinct possibility, too, when I met him 15 years ago.

I first saw him when he got into a University of Louisville basketball game. The crowd went crazy. There's something about a 500-pound basketball player that makes you stand up and cheer. He was very aware of his weight problem, and was doing something about it.

When I approached Troy with the idea of doing a story on his weight-loss battle, he was afraid I was going to make fun of him. Being obese was viewed completely differently back then. It was long before shows like "The Biggest Loser." Competitive eating wasn't even cool yet. And game announcers routinely said things like, "When his beeper goes off, people think a truck is backing up."

Despite all the jokes at his expense, he agreed to let us into his life. A lot of weight to perspire, but much more substance to admire. When he arrived in Louisville out of high school, the athletic department pulled out a scale that's never been topped. Not even by mountainous football players. The scale went up to 500 pounds. He buried it.

JOHN BOEL

No one really knows how much Troy weighed before he
started his crash weight-loss program, because by the time
the staff went out and bought what they would name "the
Troy Jackson scale," which went up to 1500 pounds, he had
already dipped below 500.

I went grocery shopping with him and watched him fill
up his cart with fruits and vegetables and healthy stuff.
He hated it. But he knew others would give him grief if
they caught him eating junk. His weight-loss crusade was
becoming very public.

He had to step on the Troy Jackson scale at the beginning
and end of every practice. I asked his conditioning coach,
Wiley Brown, what was the most weight Troy gained in a
24-hour period.

"Fifteen pounds," he said.

"No way," I replied. "How did he explain that?"

"Here's what he told me. He told me he ate a pizza."

We laughed at the inconceivability of that. Since then,
I've gained eight pounds between the end of one exhaustive
triathlon workout and the beginning of another the
following day. So, it's not hard to fathom at all that a 400-
pound man could gain 15 pounds back after a particularly
grueling, sweaty workout.

At the end of shooting our story, Troy had gone from
somewhere over 500 pounds to 370. What a statement.
Shedding 130 pounds is amazing. But Troy confided in me
that he was worried. He knew this addiction to food was
something he would be battling the rest of his life.

This amazing athlete went on to become a star on the

94

Harlem Globetrotters, as well as the And-1 Tour, but both stints were brief. He was becoming a bit of a sideshow because of his size. Every time I saw him, he was getting bigger.

Troy Jackson knew he was on the clock when it came to his battle. He only got 15 more years. Dead at the age of 35. There are so many of us who are on the clock, too, battling addictions that end lives long before the game is supposed to be over.

GOOD EVENING, I'M
RON·BURGUNDY?

A movie doesn't begin to do us justice.

"**D**amn, who typed the question mark on the teleprompter?"

That's what the news director muttered in the movie, because Ron Burgundy indeed read that sentence as a question. What kind of an idiot reads whatever is on the teleprompter, regardless of what it says? Don't news anchors even know their own name?

I've watched two different anchors actually get their own name wrong at the start of a newscast. "Good evening, I'm (another woman's name) . . . ." The producers had copied the wrong anchor's name into the newscast introduction. That's believable. The anchors read it verbatim. That's unbelievable. Maybe they saw the wrong name coming up in the teleprompter, but couldn't remember their own name.

What's worse than getting your own name wrong? How about moderating a mayoral debate, and getting the name of one of the candidates wrong. No teleprompter to blame this time. Just a script handed to me by the debate organizers. I failed to catch their error and called the independent candidate for mayor the wrong name during the introductions. He eviscerated me in front of hundreds of people, as well he should. For the next hour, I was sweating like Albert Brooks in the movie *Broadcast News*.

Sports guys aren't any better. They'll read whatever is on the teleprompter, regardless of what it says. Viewers watched one Louisville sports anchor announce, "Antoine Walker played, and sucked, during the all-star game." While viewers found it outrageous when another sports anchor referred to a close-up of a high school cheerleader's chest as "a little bust on the sidelines," I'm sure the photographer who handed him that crude script never imagined he'd read it verbatim.

Anchors don't always read whatever is in the script or on the teleprompter. A common tactic is skipping over words they don't know. That's usually necessary when anchors don't read over their scripts ahead of time. Most of the time, skipping over troublesome words works. The viewer never knows. But sometimes it turns out badly, like when a producer wrote the following tease: "Coming to a supermarket near you: irradiated meat."

One Louisville anchor froze when she got to that odd-looking word, and the tease came out like this: "Coming to a supermarket near you: . . . meat."

I've always wondered how many viewers stuck around to learn more about the appearance of meat at the grocery store.

A lot of anchors have an excuse for butchering the words in their newscast. Instead of going over the stories coming up in the next news segment, they spend their time in the commercial breaks texting, tweeting or posting comments on Facebook via the anchor desk computers or their personal devices. Spelling and grammar don't matter in those forums, and you don't have to worry about things like proper pronunciation.

News anchors are supposed to be the all-knowing godfathers of the newscast. That's hard to do for the anchors I've observed at different stations over the years who only work three or four hours a day. Often, they know less about the content than anyone in the newsroom. A high school kid asked the anchor he was job shadowing what the lead story was that she would be reading in a few minutes.

"You'll have to ask the producer," was the response.

I watched in horror as a news anchor, on the day of the Kentucky Derby at Churchill Downs, asked the head of the Visa Triple Crown the following question:

"So, what is the Triple Crown, a horse race or something?"

I'll bet that guy still tells his buddies about the time in Louisville, on Derby Day, sitting next to the Twin Spires, when a news anchor asked him if the Triple Crown is a horse race.

Then there's the Louisville anchor who asked her co-anchor a question about one of the stories in the newscast she had just finished proofreading. He immediately recognized it as one of the stories from the day before. She had clicked on the wrong computer rundown and was reviewing the previous day's newscast by mistake. That means she read over every story that she had delivered 24 hours earlier, and failed to recognize or comprehend any of it.

The all-knowing anchor concept is so important, we

were given handouts on it way back in the 1980s. Even the anchor questions to reporters were supposed to be scripted as statements, so the anchors wouldn't look like there is anything out there they don't know. Naive, stupid and right out of college, I asked, "How is the reporter supposed to answer a question that's just been answered?"

"They'll just have to expand on what the anchor said," was the answer.

For reasons like that, anchors tend to have an inflated sense of self-worth, especially with their colleagues. The reason why Ron Burgundy's line, "I'm kind of a big deal around here," is so funny, is because it's so true. At the opening of a new football stadium in Louisville, one local news anchor tried to get an interview with a coach already being interviewed by a lowly reporter from another station.

"Do you know who the f--- I am?" he yelled.

Yes, even the people who didn't know who you are can figure out exactly what you do for a living.

How do anchors get so good at the art of reading a teleprompter? That's where consultants come in. The first anchor consultant I was ever sent to told me I need to read slower. So I did. The next consultant told me to speed up. She said it's impossible to read too fast. So I read faster, with the urgency she requested. The next consultant told me to slow down. At the next consulting session, I was told to speed up. But this time, it wasn't a different consultant telling me to do something different. It was the same consultant who'd previously told me to slow down. Some of these people who are telling me how to anchor have never been an anchor. They sure sound like they know their stuff, so I always do what they say.

Perhaps the worst part of being an anchor is the cosmetic end of the business. After one of my managers told me never to wear glasses on the anchor desk, the next one ordered me to wear my dorky, round wire-rim glasses in every newscast. He said it made me look "cerebral." I already thought I was pretty smart because I never got my own name wrong. Then, when I developed a vision issue that forced me to wear my contact lenses, he made me wear my glasses as well, with clear plastic lenses. Fake glasses over blue tinted contact lenses. Nobody had a problem with the bad porn moustache.

We get so immersed in the cosmetic end of the business that we don't realize how crazy it looks to other people. Even children. When one of the many school or scout tours that come and go through TV stations stopped at my desk one day, it all hit me. After answering a couple of typical, innocuous questions, I noticed one of the elementary school-aged boys was visibly perplexed upon his return from the restroom. He raised his hand slowly.

"Why . . . is there make-up . . . in the boys bathroom?"

Everybody in the newsroom literally laughed out loud. He's right. To a boy, tackle boxes are supposed to be filled with fishing lures. Not Maybelline and Estee Lauder.

"Well," I stumbled, "some of the guys use some of that stuff so they don't look shiny and pale under the bright lights out on the set."

Good job. Got out of that one.

"Do you wear make-up?" he asked, pointing at me.

"No, not really. I just put on powder once in awhile."

"That IS make-up," everybody behind me shouted, as more laughter broke out. Anchor denial is a terrible thing.

Some anchors just can't take it anymore. One of the finest news anchors I ever worked with moved far away and became a farmer after he got fired. Another one left the business and became a minister. He told a columnist he got tired of being a "professional tattler"—telling everyone what a bunch of people did wrong every day.

While news anchoring is seldom the path to becoming a preacher, journalism is fading fast on the path to becoming a news anchor. Many years ago, my daughter brought home the official program for one of the premier pageants in this country. Each page listed each contestant's bio information, as well as her goals. One wanted to be a doctor. One wanted to be a senator. I counted 14 who wanted to be a TV news anchor. Not just any anchor. "Network" news anchor, many of them insisted. None of the 14 had any journalism or communication majors or minors on their résumés.

And that makes sense after a conversation I had recently with a pretty college girl, interested in getting a newsroom internship.

"What would you like to be someday?"

"A TV news anchor."

"Great. Have you taken lots of writing and communication courses?"

"No, but I have taken plenty of acting and modeling."

She's going to go far, even if she forgets her own name.

LETHAL DEJECTION

It's different when it's your own.

D rops of water mix with fresh black dirt and slimy earthworms searching for cover. It's not rain. It's a downpour of tears dropping into the hole I'm trying to dig in my backyard.

I've never tried to dig one this deep. Not even for some of the trees I've planted in my yard. But this hole is different. It's for my dog. Derby is scheduled for execution tomorrow.

Derby doesn't know what I'm doing. She's tied outside the tall wooden fence that surrounds my backyard. I've picked a shady spot in between two trees where she likes to go to the bathroom. The vet told us we're not supposed to bury animals on our property. I don't really know what the explanation was. Hillbillies in my old neighborhood did it. Our new neighborhood probably isn't zoned for dead animal carcasses. I wasn't listening very well after learning cancer is ravaging our pet and she is in severe pain almost all the time. If anything, I've waited too long.

So, here I am, digging a grave on a beautiful day while my dog soaks up some of the last sunshine and warm breeze she'll ever experience on this earth. I keep setting the shovel down so I can sit and cry some more. I used to make fun of Derby. Never felt close to her. But I was watching a bunch of old family videos the other night and there she was, at every important moment. This is tearing me up much worse than I expected. I can't get out of my mind a story I shot over a decade ago.

It was a profile of two long-time workers at the local Humane Society. Every day, for the previous 10 to 15 years, they had the duty of lethally injecting anywhere from a half dozen to 40 or more dogs and cats. I couldn't imagine what that was like. What that does to your senses. What that does to your outlook on life every day.

After spending time with them, it was clear they were not callous monsters. In fact, they were two of the kindest guys I've ever met. They handled the animals like coveted prizes. These pets were prizes once upon a time. But they ended up on death row. Many of them were left in the overnight deposit boxes outside by the main entrance. The workers told me all 12 of the drop boxes were often filled when they came in to work in the morning.

Pet owners don't like to look another human in the eye when they drop off their cat or dog. They don't like having to explain why their disposable pet is no longer wanted. They don't want to be informed that only one out of every six animals dropped off would be successfully adopted. The other five would have to be put down. All of the people I interviewed as they walked out truly believed their pet would be the exception. When I went back inside, I realized many of their animals were going to be dead before they got home. Unlike the city animal shelter, the Humane Society didn't have to hold animals for seven days. There's only so much room. Pets deemed "unadoptable" don't even get a last supper.

They say a dog's sense of smell is 40 times stronger than a human. It must be true. They must be able to smell death in the air. They were quivering worse than I was when they were brought in the room where they would be put down. No matter how gently the technicians stroked and spoke to them, they shook so badly they could hardly stand on all fours. The two men explained how this never gets easier, despite the fact that, by my calculations, they've done this more than 75,000 times in their careers.

We didn't have any idea how to shoot this because we didn't know what we would be allowed to show on TV. We watched in silent horror as the first injection knocked each animal out in a matter of just a few breaths. The second one brought the heart to a stop. So much involved in a life. Even a dog's life. But they died so fast. When they dropped, it was like a tree falling. The techs cradled their fall gently. I never realized how quickly life can bolt from our bodies.

Like most of the stories I've covered, I was able to drive home and put it out of my mind. But now I'm driving home to watch it one more time. This time it's my dog. We're going to pay the extra money to have the vet come to our house, because I'm still haunted by how all those quivering dogs could smell exactly what was coming.

When I pull in the driveway, my wife is sitting out on the lawn one last time with Derby. She's crying, and trying to squeeze every gust of wind and every chirping bird out of these last moments for her pet. An hour ago, I was anchoring a newscast filled with the deaths of famous people, and the only thing I mourned was the pending death of a dog.

The vet could not be nicer when he arrives, but Derby knows something is wrong. She's in too much pain to put up a fight. We place her in her bed and try to talk to her while the vet administers the chemicals. We tell her how much we love her. We tell her what a good girl she has been for us. After all these years, I think she understands the words we're using. I also think she understands this is goodbye, because we're sobbing, and she's not fighting. The life flows out of her limbs just as fast as it did for those disposable pets at the Humane Society.

The vet excuses himself as I'm sure he often does at scenes like this. Two people lying on the floor, sobbing, and clutching their dead dog. But we can't do this forever. I have to get up, bury the dog in the backyard grave, and get back to work, so I can read more stories about death at 6 P.M.

I don't think any death in the news, or in my life, has rattled me as badly as the one I just witnessed.

A MAN OF IRON

The right attitude, no matter how hard life gets

My fascination with the 140-mile-long Ironman Triathlon began back in college when the now famous race was still in its infancy. I watched, mesmerized from my dorm room, as a woman named Julie Moss stumbled, collapsed, clawed and drooled her way inch-by-inch toward the looming finish line. As she crept closer, she lost control of her bowels and soiled herself right there on TV. No one thought any less of her. In fact, her fight to the finish line is still one of the most epic struggles ever captured on camera in sports. And she didn't even win. She got passed just inches away from the line, but no one noticed.

Attempting the race's 2.4-mile swim, 112-mile bike ride, and 26-mile marathon run, all in one day, is insane, especially in typical 90-degree heat. I've finished it as fast as 12 hours and 16 minutes. I've also been rushed to the hospital after collapsing in my own puke 13 miles from the finish.

The Ironman Triathlon is a metaphor for life. We spend a long time training for life in school. No matter how well we prepare, some of us will flourish, some will simply endure, and others will stumble and fail along the way. And when we get to the finish line, we will first confess that getting there was much more difficult than we ever expected. And as with the race called life, the first-place finisher isn't necessarily the real champion.

Dick Miller doesn't seem like anyone special when I show up at his Louisville home on a hot summer day. He's 66 years old, and one of three aging athletes who have agreed to be profiled in an Ironman documentary I'm producing. To be honest, I was just looking for old people when I started calling the local folks who had signed up and paid the $500 entry fee. I already have a 67-year-old guy who has agreed to be featured, and a woman who is attempting the Ironman on her 50th birthday.

Dick is different. After crossing the finish line of one of those shorter 32-mile-long Olympic distance triathlons, he felt unusually dizzy and couldn't talk. After a series of CAT scans, they found a golf-ball sized tumor in the left side of his brain. Dick was given only two more years to live. With all the painful cancer treatments ahead, he did what any of us would do. He signed up for the Ironman Triathlon.

The fast finisher of 28 Boston Marathons also finished surgery and chemo in incredible shape. Doctors told him his impressive physical fitness accounted for that.

I'm there waiting for him in the dark, at six in the morning, when he shows up in the rain to swim in the outdoor pool at his health club. The cancer is gone, and so are all the other people at this hour. Our station news vehicle, decaled up like a Nascar machine, follows him around his neighborhood with a camera on his tail while he's jogging. And when it's time for an interview, I don't have to think of many intelligent questions. Every sentence out of his mouth is thought-provoking.

"Hey, I was told after they diagnosed the tumor that I had a short time to live. That gets a lot of things in perspective. Your family and everything."

He's going through all this training work, but he says he won't be upset if he doesn't finish the Ironman Triathlon. I believe him.

"To me, right now, every day's a gift and you have to treat it that way. And when you make decisions, you say, well, if I die tomorrow, what would I do today? And that's the way I live my life right now."

Dick Miller has to bow out of the Ironman at the 114-mile mark due to doctors' concerns over dehydration. He signs up and pays money the next day for the next year's Ironman. Again, stifling 90-plus degree heat deals another dehydration blow, forcing him out of the race. He's not crying, like the other people who cannot finish. Dick pulls his bike over and tells his wife to get the car and take him home. He feels like a winner.

"I'm lucky. I got two years free," he says to me. You see, he just passed the two-year mark of the death sentence delivered by doctors. In the race that matters, he's ahead of cancer.

When you really think about it, all of us are in a similar situation. Something is gaining on us. Cancer. Heart disease. An addiction. Something we may not even know about yet. Or maybe it's just age, and the inevitably of death. But something is gaining on us. So, how do we respond?

Dick Miller, 0 for 2 in the Ironman, responds by signing up again for a third try next year.

We're all on the clock. But Dick Miller refuses to call a time out. He's squeezing out every second. And when the buzzer does eventually sound, he already won a long time ago.

What's our excuse?

IN THE NEWS

INSTITUTIONALIZED

A Thanksgiving trip over the river and through the woods

Asickening feeling compresses my gut as I drive by the scene of the crime. I haven't been here in 25 years. This is where it all exploded. Downing 64-ounce beer bongs. Spewing stomach contents. Losing bowel control for good measure.

What are the odds on me having to pass right by my college dorm on the way to a northwoods rehab dorm where I'm checking myself in for alcoholism treatment. There's no way that's a coincidence. This is the way God speaks to people.

For the second time in a little over two years, I've been busted for DUI. For the second time, the TV station where I worked reported my arrest and posted my mug shot on its newscasts. For the first time in my life, I got fired.

Both DUIs came the same way: leaving a Kentucky horse track after a day of drinking and winning and celebrating with the same friends. Nobody is that dumb. Despite the alcohol assessment two years ago by a licensed counselor that found me "not alcohol dependent," now I know I need help.

I picked the same treatment center that my brother-in-law went to 20 years ago. He came here three different times for alcoholism treatment and then put a 44-magnum in his mouth to end the pain of this disease. The first place they send me is to a psychologist because they can see I'm suicidal. My dad is either too nervous or too embarrassed to come in the facility, but my mom talks him into entering. Without hesitation, they write a check, lending us thousands of dollars to help pay the more than $5,000 that my insurance won't pay. For many people at a point like this in life, cost is no object. It is for me. I'm a nosy journalist. I have to ask. They tell me the cost of 28 days of treatment is now up to $28,000. For a thousand dollars a day, I had better come out of here the happiest teetotaler on earth.

Once they're reasonably sure I won't kill myself, they send me to the medical unit for the standard 24-hour detox. I don't need it, blowing a .000 for the first time in a long time.

I'm surrounded by shuffling zombies. It's *Night of the Living Dead*, but it's in color. My roommate is moaning "Help me" from his bed when I walk in. I don't know whether I feel more like Jack Nicholson in *One Flew Over The Cuckoo's Nest*, or like Jack Nicholson in *The Shining*. A heavy, wet snow is falling outside, the first of several snowstorms that will bury us over the next month. I'm already buried by the avalanche that just happened in my life.

After 24 hours in detox, I'm escorted to the unit where I'll be spending the next four weeks. Many of the guys are winding up the evening by watching a movie in the lounge.

"What are you watching?" I ask.

The Hangover, they reply.

Damn. No kidding. They're actually watching *The Hangover*. I try an icebreaker.

"Does anyone find it odd that a bunch of alcoholics and drug addicts in rehab are watching *The Hangover*?" Everybody smiles. Nobody finds it strange.

"Well, it's a movie about the consequences of over-indulging," one of the guys says. Alcoholics can rationalize anything.

"True," I reply, "but if I walked past the sex addiction wing right now, would they be watching porn?"

I get laughs off that line. It's the last time I'll laugh for weeks. Funny how the funniest movie I've ever watched is not remotely interesting in rehab.

CELEBRITY REHAB
WITHOUT DR. DREW

No Charlie or Lindsay when you need them

When your life has crash-landed, and you hurriedly pack for rehab, it's surprising what you throw in the suitcase. I have plenty of pairs of shorts in Minnesota, where it's below freezing before Halloween. I packed the jersey of my favorite NFL quarterback who, I'm told, was in this very unit kicking his addiction. I'm so glad my family threw photographs in my suitcase. As I set them out, one-by-one, I see a common theme. I remember every one of these moments spanning the past decade, and in every photo, I'm horrified to realize I had been drinking.

As a journalist fresh out of college, my first investigative report was on an alcohol treatment center. Now I'm in one. The first thing I learn is that this is going to be nothing like my favorite TV show, "Celebrity Rehab with Dr. Drew." No lounging around the pool verbally sparring with spoiled babies. Beginning at 6:30, a tightly-scripted 14-hour day is printed out in individual schedules. You get fined if your bed is not made right or a light is left on. Chores are assigned weekly. I get garbage duty.

The counselors don't remotely resemble Dr. Drew. They're all recovering addicts or alcoholics and they cannot be fooled. One of them was a meth-head. He says he walked in on two guys, dead of a meth overdose, and responded like any normal human being would—by going through their pockets in case they had any more unused drugs.

Compassion seems to be lacking in everyone's stories. A heroin junkie, shipped in here by bus without any shoes on, fondly describes something they call the "Dead Junkie House." It's an abandoned house where all the heroin addicts in town went to shoot up over the years. One of them keeled over and died of an overdose with the needle still sticking out of his arm. Drug addicts came and went for days, months and years. Nobody did anything. The dead junkie decomposed right in front of them. Over time, the needle got rusty. But the story never gets old.

There are 18 guys in my unit. Talk about diversity. A federal judge. A stand-up comedian. A professional motorcycle racer. A drug dealer who was making $50,000 a month. A golf course superintendent who was knocking down a case of beer a day. An oxycontin fiend who got mugged three different times in one night trying to score some in Chicago. And a staggering number of college kids who are already in rehab.

Nobody is here because he thought it was high time to get cleaned up. Every person is here because of a cataclysmic event in life. An arrest. A divorce. A lost job. Only one man on the unit is here because of an "intervention." His family paid a professional interventionist $5,000 to get him here. I asked him what they got for $5,000. He said the man drove him to the airport, flew with him, and then followed the shuttle from the airport to the rehab center. Apparently they were worried he might open the door on the moving shuttle van and make a break for freedom across a field. My favorite detail: the interventionist bought him a beer at the airport. Professional interventionist sounds like a fun, lucrative job.

Almost every day, a new guy stumbles in and a 28-day veteran graduates and heads back to reality. The difference between the incoming and outgoing flights is amazing to me, so I have some hope.

But I'm also surrounded by several blowhards who know everything. Problem is, they're back in treatment for the third or fourth time, clearly not practicing what they preach.

One of the first things we have to do is take a battery of tests. The only one I recognize is the MMPI, which is supposed to gauge my mental health by asking me questions like, "Have you ever wanted to be a girl?" A man next to me, who is dressed like a woman, is taking the same test. I wonder how she/he answered.

While I have my doubts, these tests turn out to be more than accurate. My psychologist tells me I scored off the chart for depression, anxiety and shame. I used to score well on tests in math, reading and writing.

The first time I pick up a newspaper, there's a big feature story on the retirement of a popular local news anchor I idolized in college. In fact, I decided to get into broadcast journalism because of his great investigative reports I watched while belting down bottles of Buckhorn beer in my dorm. One thing I didn't know about him until this newspaper feature: he got sent to rehab by his employer after alcohol swallowed him up. Funny how God keeps sending me signals.

Every morning after our meditation and prayer session, I go downstairs to the laundry room where no one can see me cry, and the dryer can drown out my sobbing. I'm a thousand miles away from friends and family at holiday time. I've been publicly crucified in the media. Lost my job. Killed my career. Humiliated my family. I can't imagine being humbled any lower. But when my peer reviews are read to me at the halfway point of my stay, I get ripped for "grandiosity." Most of them think I'm Ron Burgundy, the big-shot news anchor, who's too cool for everyone else. They think I'm a self-absorbed, bragging blowhard who's judgmental, superficial and doesn't care about anyone else.

I'm shocked.

Then I realize they nailed it.

REVELATIONS

What makes me tick is what made me sick.

F or as long as I can remember, I was always the guy who made fun of the victims in celebrity sexual assault cases or, at the very least, poked holes in their stories.

Excuse me. "Alleged" victim is how I referred to each when re-writing scripts.

Seriously, are you telling me Kobe raped a woman with no weapon, on a bum knee, right after surgery? Big Ben raped a woman in a public restroom, with no weapon, and she didn't resist because she said he was in a bad mood? I was the only reporter covering the Tyson rape trial in Indianapolis who argued his innocence long after he was convicted.

Decades later, when victims started coming forward in Louisville's priest sex abuse lawsuits, I was the first to cast stones. I was sexually abused as a kid. So were lots of people. Get over it.

So, it comes as no surprise that our treatment counselors, in an effort to scare the guys away from the girls, constantly warn us that "95 percent" of the female addicts and

FAMILY MATTERS

Rehab's version of the Springer show

The first person stands up to introduce himself. He breaks down before he can get to his last name. The gray-haired gentleman apologizes and sits down. His wife gets up and crumbles before she can finish. Wow. This is way more intense than the Packers–Vikings game I'm missing right now.

There are about 40 people sitting in a circle. All we have to do is say our name, where we live, and why we're here. Half of the people in this circle are patients here. The other half are family members of patients. It's easy to tell the family members. They're the ones with boxes of Kleenex in their laps. And they're the ones who act like they're at a funeral.

This special three-day program in rehab purposely puts together people suffering from addiction and the people suffering because of us. Patients are not allowed to take this program at the same time as their own family members. This way, there's no friction. More importantly, this way I get to see more objectively what my disease does to moms, dads, wives and children, without the emotional attachment of having my family in the room.

As soon as we break up into smaller groups, I can see these family members are incredibly angry. Wives moving out. Husbands filing divorce papers. Parents disowning children. Children disowning parents. They're all convinced personal weakness is what drives our behavior. They think we lack discipline. We've become bad people. That's what we thought, too.

So the treatment center gives the family members a crash course on the same things we're learning. We're not bad people. We're good people with a bad disease. A chronic, progressive, fatal disease that will kill us if we don't follow a recovery program. We either inherited the biological drive to use drugs or alcohol to medicate our minds or we manufactured it through prolonged use. They watch many of the same videos, brain scans and lectures as we do. They're dying to ask us difficult questions every chance they get. Tougher questions than I've ever posed in any interviews I've done as a journalist. Without any prodding, they offer up sensitive details of their lives without hesitation. Oprah would be jealous of how fast they're gushing details. A man from Florida who makes the money and raises the kids while his wife raises the bottle and passes out every day at home. A teenager who has watched every member of her family fall prey to addiction. Both of her parents and all of her brothers and sisters. She can't figure out why she's different, but she's the one who wants to commit suicide.

On one hand, these personal exchanges make me feel much better about myself. I can see I was a much more functional alcoholic than any of the guys these bitter wives are describing. They drank in the morning. They drank at work. They had bottles hidden all over the house. In fact, their wives can't believe I was able to accomplish as much as I did in that kind of condition. But on the other hand, when they start sobbing multiple times in a ten-minute conversation, I can see how terribly we've wrecked their lives. It's a great motivation. We owe it to these people to get better. I'll do whatever it takes.

Every story is the same from the family members: multiple failures when it comes to staying sober. These people have put up with way too much crap from their loved ones. I would have been gone long ago. But they're still sticking around. Come to think of it, so is my family.

My wife has already married me twice. I don't think there will be a third time. She also went to college in Wisconsin, so she knows how to drink. In fact, I was horrified by what I often saw at her house parties. Teams of two, assigned their own keg of beer. First pair to polish off the keg won. Beer bongs were encouraged. Puking was allowed. It's the only way to keep clearing enough room to get a keg of beer through the human body. But Brenda didn't turn out like me. Neither did her friends. They all knew where to draw the line.

After three days of education and interrogation, the family members who came in here full of rage are now feeling sorry for us. We're the ones filled with anger when they leave. Anger at ourselves for how horribly we've devastated our families in ways we never realized.

My wife emerged from this family program a week ago a completely different person. She's glowing now. Beaming with smiles. The guys in my unit can't believe her transformation. She knows exactly when I need support and when I need distance. "Detach, with love," is what they're taught. My recovery is my responsibility now. I fought her every step of the way when she said she wanted to come back up here and take part in this program. I was wrong again. It's going to be immeasurably helpful. The list of things I've been wrong about continues to grow.

Maybe it's the journalist in me. Or maybe it's the Jerry Springer in me. But after spending so much time getting to know these devoted family members, I can't wait to see who they're actually married to in here. That opportunity only comes when the patients are allowed to sit with their spouses and children at the evening lecture. The classy, leggy, tall blonde I've gotten to know well slices through the crowd to get to a ponytailed, haggard, nasty-looking dude. She must be getting directions to where her husband is sitting. Wait. That is her husband. No way. I need some I.D. The fit, tanned, wealthy husband from Florida must be married to a babe. But the woman he's kissing is a weathered wreck. Face drawn. Bags under her eyes. Beer gut. Not remotely pretty. Pretty shocking, over and over, as I marvel at the love connections.

Wait a minute. Who do I think I am? Look at me in the

mirror. Bloated. Disfigured face. Red eyes. Unshaven face. Greasy hair. Wrinkled sweat pants. I've never looked worse. I guarantee others are having the same reaction I just had when they see my wife walk up and hug me.

"Is she really married to that guy? What does she see in him?"

What do they see in any of us?

POPULAR CULTURE

They can't get enough of us.

C rack open the paper here in rehab and there's a big feature section spread on Charlie Sheen's downward spiral. Of course, they have to throw in a little Lindsay Lohan, Mel Gibson and Robert Downey, Jr., too.

Back at home, the local media bloggers are having a field day on the Internet. At least one of them is setting records by writing about me. Everything he publishes, from the arrest to the rehab trip, attracts exponentially more hits than any of the stories about things that actually affect his readers' lives.

It's fascinating. People love to revel in the downfall of others. The only thing separating my disease from all the other guys with me in rehab is the excuse that I'm a "public figure." I read a teleprompter on TV. Charlie Sheen plays an irresponsible, intoxicated, immature character on TV, so the same frat boy behavior in real life is more excusable, and a must-read.

The dissection of his disease goes off the deep end. Experts weigh in on how horrible a father Sheen must be. Others rant about how much more disgusted people would be if this was all happening to a woman. I don't really understand that one. These same people will be blasting Lindsay Lohan tomorrow.

Psychiatrists explain how addicts tend to be highly functional, so Sheen has been able to pull this off for a long time. That's precisely why I didn't believe I was an alcoholic. I'm out there doing triathlons every other weekend and pulling down handfuls of Emmy awards every year, so I can't be an addict.

The experts in the newspaper point out addicts often times need several stints in rehab. Makes sense to me. The treatment center I'm in claims one-third of the people who come here eventually come back in for treatment again. Aerosmith's Steven Tyler blew that away with eight trips. No way that's happening to me. I'm from Kentucky, so I'm going to be "one and done."

The story in the paper details how TV executives are doing everything possible to get Sheen back even though it's costing millions of dollars. His show draws in 14 million viewers every week. When he's in rehab, even the re-runs do well.

Sheen rips the media for the focus on his personal life, calling all this coverage "pathetic." He points out there's a war going on and Egypt is burning. There's also a story in the paper today on a college coach donating a kidney to save the life of a freshman player on the team. It's the most wonderful and compelling story of the day by far. But I'll get to it in a minute. I have to get back to this incredible story involving an outrageous actor, his night with a porn star and piles of cocaine.

THE ADJUSTMENT BUREAU

Holiday spirits of a different flavor

I always loved watching *Scrooge* over the holidays. Now I'm living it. I came in here a broken, miserable person. In order to change me, they're haunting me at Christmas time with constant visits from the ghosts of John's past, John's present, and John's future.

One of my first assignments is to re-examine my life, in five-year chunks, and assess my alcohol use along the way. By my 16th birthday, I was already chugging Mogen David 20/20 and throwing it all back up. In college, I went to house parties with a beer bong holstered in my belt loop. Every Friday and Saturday night, for four years, I paid two dollars at the door for all I could drink. They lost badly on that deal. My beer bong held up to 64 ounces. One night, after downing a couple of 64-ouncers a few minutes apart, I shook uncontrollably. The next week, I read where a college student in Illinois died after doing a big beer bong at a party. He started shaking uncontrollably and went into alcohol shock.

How scary. So, I reduced beer bong portions to 48 ounces. The experts here in rehab say if you can't predict the outcome when you start drinking, then you're alcoholic. As I examine my past, I can't ever remember a sustained period of time where I drank one or two at night and capped it at that. When I drink, something happens to me that doesn't happen to other people. They say I have a disease of the mind and body. My mind craves alcohol when it's not in me, and I'm powerless over alcohol when I start pouring it in my body.

They say alcoholics and addicts often are born with exceedingly low levels of dopamine and serotonin in the brain, and when we discover how to boost those levels with booze or drugs, the game is on.

Three times a day, for 28 days, lecturers help us examine our past, present and future, by sharing their past and present, and making sobriety their future. They know all of us have been lying, scheming or faking to get our fix, pill or drink.

"There is no real joy in a fake life," one says. "When you operate on a lie, you run into the truth."

Fortunately for me, I never ran into anyone or anything while driving drunk. I don't understand why I keep driving when I've been drinking. They explain the decision-making part of the brain is bypassed when people with this disease start drinking. They show brain scans that reveal how wildly our pathways have been chemically altered. That's why they call it "The Hijacked Brain." Addiction is not a voluntary behavior. I couldn't keep my promises to stop because my brain is chemically altered with a powerful biological drive to want to use alcohol to feel better.

The ghost of John's past is not as merciless as the ghost of John's present. From the counselors to the patients, everybody here is brutally honest. They have to be. Our lives are on the line. According to them, I make fun of people. I think I'm better than everybody else. I'm selfish. I throw my credentials and accomplishments around. I'm always too busy for anyone else's problems. I'm intolerant, arrogant, and I isolate myself.

When one or two people accuse me of things like that, I can explain it away. When a jury of my peers unanimously convicts me on all counts, it's impossible to deny. Only about half of the in-patient experience here deals with overcoming addiction. The other half is spent flushing out and trying to remove our character defects. Clearly, I have a lot of homework. To get the ball rolling, they make me take long walks with others and talk about these issues.

My first walk is at night on a trail in the woods during another round of the 40 inches of snow that falls during my stay. A stand-up comedian half my age knows more about me in two weeks than I apparently know about myself. I've brushed aside so many people like him in my life. All they've wanted is to be my friend and help me. The snow keeps falling. My dopamine and serotonin levels are rising naturally, without a boost from alcohol. And it feels good to finally feel good.

The ghost of John's future reveals himself daily in many ways. If I continue on this course, I see what's ahead through the unbelievable stories shared by many of the speakers. One man went to treatment 17 times. One woman's father went to rehab 26 times before he died of his disease. I see my future in the worn, limping, alcohol-soaked old men who have to hit the medical station several times a day because of what decades of drinking did to their bodies. Many of these people literally lost everything. The future looks brighter after the messages of dozens of speakers who've done far worse and were further gone than I am. Yet after decades of sobriety, they're higher on life than I've ever been. They convince me I can't change what happened. I can't change other people. I can't even change my disease. But I can change me.

The stats on the future aren't exactly encouraging, even at a highly successful treatment center like this. Or maybe they are, depending on your perspective. One-third of the patients who leave here remain abstinent for the rest of their lives. Another third require more than one trip to treatment before becoming abstinent. And the final third will resume drinking and die of their disease. There are no diplomas handed out. We're never cured.

As each day goes by, I begin to understand this concept of concentrating only on the next 24 hours. If I "do the next right thing" in every decision I make all day long, then when I wake up tomorrow I'll have no regrets about yesterday. If I feel better about myself, I will have eliminated one big reason to drink. Beyond that, the experts say I only have to change one thing: everything. Everything from my playgrounds to my playmates.

While Scrooge woke up on Christmas morning a giddy, changed man, I wake up at 4 A.M. for no apparent reason on my last night in rehab. As I stare into the darkness through the glass patio door next to my bed, my eyes eventually assemble a surreal image in front of me. Just a few feet away is a towering buck. Bigger than life. That's because the deer is standing up on his hind legs. He's standing erect so he can extend high enough to eat the berries way up in a tree. He shuffles left and right like a kid on stilts when he has to maneuver for more food. I've done a lot of deer hunting and I've never seen or heard of anything like this. He's walking around on two legs like a human. He has no idea I'm watching him.

I think God called him up to my window and woke me up to teach me a lesson. Sometimes we have to get out of our comfort zone. Sometimes, when the snow gets deep and life gets hard, we have to reach really high for the good stuff.

A few hours later, I take my last walk at the treatment center. An ultra-light snow is slowly falling to the ground. The flakes are so tiny and wispy, it looks like they're floating down in slow motion. I remember my first day here, and many other days, when large, wet flakes were bombarding me out here like Frisbees.

Like these miniature snowflakes, I feel like the weight of the world has been lifted off me over these 28 days. I see where I've been. How I got here. How I need to change. Where I need to go from here. And what will happen if I don't. The three spirits did their job. I have enough time to make amends to the people I've hurt and someday help others. I stop and sit on a bench donated by the family of a man who committed suicide because of his addiction. I remember my brother-in-law, who did the same thing after coming here. As the tears roll down my frozen cheeks, I thank God for the best month of my life, at the worst time of my life.

Then, like a scene in a movie, the old man who drives the shuttle back to the airport hands me my suitcase at the gate. In a handshake moment he must repeat thousands of times, he pauses, and looks me straight in the eye.

"Have a great life."

The snow is falling harder. His warm smile just got softer.

"I think I will now. Thank you."

I can't wait to get home. A check of my watch. There's still enough time to get the Christmas lights up.

DONE-EMPLOYMENT OFFICE

Begging for dollars the modern day way

"Hey, question for you," says a big NFL-sized guy who walks right up to me, "Has anyone ever told you that you look just like that John Boel guy on TV?"

"That's me. I'm John."

"What the hell are you doing in here?" he asks, dumbfounded. We're standing in the unemployment office.

"I got fired. I'm unemployed."

"Really? Why?"

"I got busted for DUI. It's been all over the news."

"Oh, man, I'm sorry," he says, pointing to a bunch of people. "All of us sitting over there were saying you look like the TV newsman, but we didn't think it was really you."

Yes, it's me, standing at the back of a line snaking around the periphery of a room more depressing than a funeral parlor. Fathers feel like failures. Snot runs down the faces of whining children who've been here for hours. Mom can't afford a babysitter while she fights for her paltry share of the money we're borrowing from China to help in the worst unemployment crisis in decades. The line is progressing at a rate of one person every three or four minutes. At this rate, I won't get up there for two hours.

"You got to be prayed-up when you come in here," says a woman behind me who read my mind.

"You John Boel, ain't you?" says the elderly woman in front of me. "I feel so bad for you. I loved watching you on the news."

Her voice is soothing, compassionate, motherly. She offers up her story to try to make me feel better.

"I was making $19 an hour when I got laid off two years ago. We knew it was coming. Our business relied on Ford. When Ford got hit, we got hit. You'll probably get the max like me: $783 after taxes, every two weeks."

As I try to hide my face from the people streaming by and staring at me, she continues telling me how lucky she's been.

"I'm blessed. My family has never gone hungry. You just figure out a way to make it."

I explain to her my unemployment has been denied and I'm appealing. I start telling this total stranger with a warm smile how depressed I am. Instead of working on speeches, my sixth grade, class president daughter has to explain to her friends how her dad lost his job and ended up in the news. One night, I overheard her explaining to a friend why she couldn't have something she wanted at the store.

"My mom is the only one who has a job now, and we barely have enough money to get us through the week."

A devastating thing for a dad to hear. Fathers are supposed to be providers. I can't even provide her with a ride to school. My sister is hurting too right now. A day care teacher barely beating minimum wage, her hours have been cut to 30 per week. The state cut her husband's disability pay in half. I was supplementing their income before I lost my job. Now all I can do is watch them suffer and it's my fault. My new friend in line can tell where my mind is right now. She surprises me with a stern look on her face.

"Don't you even think about giving up. Your life was bought at a price. Don't ever forget that. God is always with you."

Tears crawl out of my eyes. The line crawls forward. People around me say it's nothing like yesterday's wait. Two hours after I walked in, I get sent to a room where a nice worker outlines the unemployment process for those of us who are here for the first time.

"I know none of you want to be here," he says. "Normally I ask for questions right now, and I always say there's no question I haven't heard before. But just a little while ago, I had a first. A woman asked me how long she has to be on unemployment before she earns a week of vacation pay."

Six of us stare at him in stunned silence.

"She was not kidding. She was totally serious," he adds.

Complicating our financial matters, my wife insists on continuing to tithe at church. Ten percent of what we're bringing in every month, regardless of how much it is. Regardless of how much life hurts. I've been trying to talk her out of it. After all, here I am, groveling for unemployment assistance. My sister could use help. Fiscally, I can think of many reasons why tithing doesn't make sense right now. Spiritually, I know my wife is right. I can already think of blessings we've received that appeared to come out of nowhere.

Months later, a letter arrives in the mail. My appeal has been successful. The checks are in the mail, going all the way back to my first week of unemployment. Another unanticipated blessing.

HYPOCRISY

What's really going on in our lives, while we judge others?

J ust my luck. Or maybe it's appropriate irony. Either way, my attorney just called and told me he has to start over on my case negotiation. That's because the woman who was prosecuting me for my DUI-2nd charge just got arrested and fired. It appears she crashed her car into a police cruiser, took off, and stopped on railroad tracks. After the cop moved her car out of the way of an oncoming train, he jailed her for DUI. She reportedly blew a 0.23.

I'd like to laugh at that hypocrisy, but I'm worse.

I got a public school bus driver fired by catching him drinking and driving right before picking up the kids and was driving my own family around hours later, after downing several beers.

I completed an investigation of a guy with 11 DUIs, still beating the system, and then promptly went out and got my own DUI.

And, worst of all, I was one of the reporters assigned to cover the 1989 trial involving the worst drunk driving tragedy in U.S. history. A school bus full of sleeping children slammed head-on into a pickup truck at 55 miles per hour. The kids were coming home from a fun day at an amusement park. The drunken pickup driver was trying to go home after a long day of drinking. But he was going the wrong way on a dark, winding stretch of Interstate 71. His name was Larry Mahoney. He survived the crash. They always do.

But 24 children and three adults died in the raging fire that erupted when a spring punctured the unprotected gas tank. Many of the 40 who survived had horrible, disfiguring burns. I listened to them testify for weeks, describing how they got out. With the front exit blocked by fire, they had to claw through the thick, black smoke to get to the rear exit. In the way, dozens of screaming, choking children, literally stacked on top of each other, trapped in the clogged doorway.

I never understood "survival of the fittest" until I heard the survivors describe how they blindly, desperately climbed over the mountain of children and squeezed out the very top of the doorway. After listening to 124 witnesses, jurors had a compelling question to decide. What kind of punishment does someone deserve who kills 27 people, and maims many others, in a drunk driving crash? For the victim's families, that would be 27 life terms. But a lot of people spend only a few months in jail for killing someone in a DUI crash.

The defense tried to blame the bus. Nobody died from the impact of the crash. The gas tank was not protected. The seats burned too fast. Mahoney wept several times.

Just a couple of days before Christmas, the jury refused to call it murder. And they were so confused at the verdict options, they ended up giving Mahoney more time for the people he injured than the people he killed. When he walked out of prison in 1999 with six years knocked off for good behavior, he'd served nearly 11 years. That comes out to about five months for each person killed.

The victims' families were devastated and, by the end of the emotional trial, I was extremely ill. I had to undergo numerous medical tests. Doctors thought I had Crohn's disease or colitis. They never did figure it out.

But now I think I know what was wrong with me. I was suffering from early-stage alcoholism, and confronting the horrors of drinking and driving every day for six weeks literally made me sick.

People were outraged when one of the school teachers, who lost several students in the crash, went out and got busted for drunk driving.

People snickered when Mahoney's attorney went out and got busted for DUI.

I wonder how Larry Mahoney reacted when he read that the reporter who covered his trial 20 years ago just got fired after another DUI.

Mahoney's blood alcohol level was .21 percent. That's only a couple sips higher than mine was recently. I was right there. Right at his trial. Right at his blood alcohol concentration. And right out on the interstate, behind the wheel, as drunk as he was, where I could have killed people too.

The alcoholic mind has the uncanny ability to edit out what it doesn't want to remember.

AN ANGEL

The prodigal son has a sister.

Three months into my DUI disaster, I'm still sober, 30 pounds lighter, can't remember feeling this healthy, and people are amazed at my transformation.

I hide it well. Truth is, I don't want to be alive any more. Several times a day, the horrible realization bombards my brain that this is not a dream. There are no more mulligans.

Speakers at the recovery program meetings I attend several times a week are always talking about the "consequences" they've suffered because of their drinking. It makes me realize I've managed to get out of just about everything I've done wrong in my life. When they hauled a hundred of my friends down to the police station from a keg party at a city councilwoman's house, I escaped with a fake ID. When a college dorm room full of us got busted for smoking dope, we got it dropped down to disorderly conduct. When I was accused of drunk driving a few feet from my driveway long ago, my attorney made it go away. Cops even gave me a ride home one night when my breath test was hovering a couple of sips under the legal limit.

This time it's different. Two bad DUIs in two years. Two public crucifixions. A struggle to get out of bed in the morning after not sleeping all night. Paralyzed by panic attacks. Filled with fear. There is no joy in anything. Not the Badgers in the Rose Bowl. Not even the Packers winning the Super Bowl. I cry every day. Not the wimpy kind. The kind that ruptures blood vessels in the nose. The last time I laughed seems like never. I contemplate suicide often. I've lined up the sheets. I've inventoried the stockpiled pills. But the life insurance won't pay. My family would be devastated. And I'm too much of a coward. The two most cherished awards I've ever received are now over 30 years old. "Best Attitude" on the swim team. And the "Coach's Award" in football, for the player who tries the hardest. But for the first time in my life, I have the worst attitude, and I'm tired of trying.

Then my telephone rings. A voice filled with joy is on the other end. It's my sister.

Handicapped since birth with a rare disease, she's had a life full of people making fun of her. She's a severe diabetic. Works with kids but can't have her own. Makes $17,000 a year. Never been able to run. Never went to prom. Never has much money. Hates accepting our assistance.

But she's always in a good mood. The highlight of her week is grocery shopping, a movie rental, or a healthy blood-sugar reading. A trip to Olive Garden makes her month.

Ever since I was a little boy, sitting for hours in the waiting room for her at Mayo Clinic, I've always felt guilty. Why did God bless me with so much, while my sister has been dealt every bad card in the deck? Why doesn't something good happen to her, just once? Why do I get so many blessings that I don't deserve?

I keep struggling with these questions. I keep screwing up and feeling sorry for myself. Then the phone rings and pure joy flows from the other end. Jenny had a great day. One of the three-year-olds she was watching at day-care hugged her and said she loved her.

Truth is, people like Jenny are here for people like me. When it comes to what's important in life, she gets it. And she gives it away at just the right times.

ANYTHING GOES

Enabling the haters brings out the worst in us.

I t never ends. Another story on me in the local media. A popular Internet blogger reports I was "allegedly spotted" having lunch with the general manager of a Louisville TV station. It's followed by a bunch of speculation and open-ended questions. I'm news even when I'm not doing anything newsworthy. I'm news even when I'm no longer a news anchor.

In the old days, not that long ago, you had an opportunity to comment on the news or the coverage of the news. All you had to do to qualify was give them your name and where you live. Accountability was important in journalism, on both sides of the fence. My name is on the product. Your name should be on your criticism of the product. Seems obvious.

But that basic principle started slipping away in Louisville back in the '90s when a media critic popped up who called himself "Ed Woodward." The weekly publication that ran his column wouldn't reveal his identity. He insisted he needed to operate anonymously so he could maintain his network of sources. If you were jealous of someone in your newsroom or secretly hated a coworker, you could stab the person in the back by dishing up some dirt to "Ed" and he could lay it all out there for everyone to see. Because a columnist isn't bound by the same rules as a journalist, "Ed" didn't have to get the other side of any of those stories. Brilliant scheme. Evil, too.

When the Internet media bloggers came along, most identified themselves, but they provided a "comment" forum for cowards to lob all kinds of hate without anyone knowing their identity. Anything goes, unless the bloggers get mad or get criticized. Then they can delete comments or expose the identities of the people they don't like. It has spun so confusingly out of control that one of the local bloggers who provides a forum for anonymous cowards to rip people actually filed a lawsuit against an anonymous coward who popped up on the Internet and started ripping him.

A staggering number of people have pounced on the opportunity to take out their frustrations on someone else, with no accountability or recourse. It's so popular, newspapers followed suit in their online comment sections. The same newspapers that used to have identification rules. When my best friend's father was struck from behind by a van and killed while riding his bike across the Clark Memorial Bridge, the comment section of the newspaper blew up with criticism of the victim. Yes, the dead grandfather who was pedalling his way from work to his granddaughter's birthday party. Chips Cronen was following every rule of the road: riding with traffic on the far right side of his lane, using hand signals and wearing a helmet. But he was assailed in the comment section by the army of bike haters out there who accused him of being on a stupid suicide mission because he wasn't riding on the sidewalk. Riding on the sidewalk is against the law, but that didn't matter to them. Cronen's family got to read all the anonymous hate while they were planning a funeral for one of the finer people in our community.

But I've noticed a strange irony in all of this. The most vicious anonymous stone throwers on these blog sites are not the viewers, but the journalists themselves. I guess it makes perfect sense after what we witnessed from the "Ed Woodward" days.

I know a newsroom manager who was devastated by disparaging comments posted about her on one of these blog sites. She isn't a public figure, and some of the stuff was very personal. She could tell some of the comments came from people in her newsroom whom she had helped out during hard times. A very talented and hard-working African-American colleague of mine was roasted by postings that played the race card. And just about the time that I was ready to dismiss all of this as harmless banter, one of these blog comment postings led to a Louisville news anchor losing his job.

Anonymous hate rains down in daily e-mails, too. I had always assumed it was coming from viewers. The most hate-filled disembowelment of me ever, personally and professionally (and that's quite an achievement), came from an e-mail that had a Bible study group address. Upon fascinating to listen to the exchanges between the multi-DUI guys and the counselor.

"How many DUIs is this?" he asks.

"My second one," a bearded, middle-aged man in hunting camo replies.

"Well, clearly, you didn't learn anything from all the counseling after your first one. Where did you go for that?"

"Here," he responds.

Oops. That hurts. So the counselor embarks on a mission to see if anyone is learning anything in these sessions. One by one, he asks the students if they're using moderation or abstinence to prevent another DUI. One by one, they answer "moderation." One guy says he's down to five beers, four nights a week. The next guy still drinks every night, but he claims he doesn't leave the house. Many of them claim they can stop when they want, but they can't recall the last time they went a week without drinking.

A stat pops back into my mind from rehab: 20 million people in this country suffer from alcoholism or drug addiction, but only one-half of one percent are doing anything about it. Now I believe it.

When it's my turn to talk, I tell them I went to rehab and realized I'm an alcoholic, so I have to choose abstinence. No one is amused when I say it sounds like all of them are trying to rationalize and minimize their alcoholism. I sound like Dr. Phil now. I need to shut up.

Everywhere I go, I see widespread misunderstanding of this disease. But from time to time, something happens that restores hope for those of us who are struggling. When the news breaks that a defensive back for the University of Louisville football team just got his second DUI in six months, everyone assumes he's gone. He's no star, and he blew right around .19 both times. But Coach Charlie Strong announces he will not be punting his player off the team. He will remain on scholarship and the school will get him the help he needs.

"Our major concern right now is to help him tackle what he is fighting right now, and that is the issue of alcoholism," Strong tells reporters. A web poll after the story shows 86 percent of the voters agree with the decision not to dismiss him from the team.

Occasionally in my recovery meetings, someone announces the suicide of a member. Often in my counseling sessions, somebody is dealing with suicidal thoughts. Today, a woman has counselors convinced she's really going to kill herself. I decide to admit I've been thinking a lot about suicide. I can't pull it off because I'm a coward. But I don't want to live anymore. The public embarrassment and shame pelting me and my family for months has not let up. Just about everyone in this room knows everything about my arrest and firing.

Instead of feeling sorry for me like the others here do, the recovering addict leading today's session goes on the attack. He explains why suicide is the by-product of ego. It's selfishness. All about me. And he offers up something that finally changes my outlook. Yes, I'm a public figure. Yes, everybody knows my sad story. But because of that, I have an opportunity that every other person in this room will never get. I have a chance to change lives by what I do now.

If you think about it, every crisis is really an opportunity. What if I fail? Better yet, what if I succeed? That's a pretty good reason to live.

I never liked counseling, until today.

LIFE IN THE SLOW LANE

The most under-appreciated card on earth

I used to be on the bus. Now I'm in it.

I hid in embarrassment years ago when my mom made the driver stop so she could snap a picture of me and the rest of the news team draped down the side of these huge public transit buses. I'm trying to hide again, this time because I have to ride the bus. My driver's license is suspended for a year. I'm too ashamed to ask most of my friends for a ride. They couldn't take me anyway. They have jobs. So does my wife.

Fortunately, it's winter. So I wear a coat with a big hood and pull it up over my head gangsta-style. It's only a buck fifty round trip? That's half of what the gas would have cost me.

It's brutally cold outside. Fortunately, the bus is on time, down to the minute. Transfers are on time. The driver is helpful and friendly. The bus is not filled with thugs and lowlifes, as I presumed. Actually, I might qualify as the lowest life on board.

I feel bad. I did several investigations following public transit and school buses around, catching the drivers doing things wrong. Speeding, blowing stop lights and, most recently, I recorded old, poor people having to wait for hours in the heat to be transported to and from medical treatment like dialysis.

Now, the former investigative reporter is relying on buses to get around town. Months go by. They're always on time, so I'm always on time. The transportation grid is comprehensive. I can go anywhere fairly easily. The ridership is made up of many more professional people and students than I imagined. People on board pitch in to help everyone from the handicapped to the Mexicans who just arrived, don't speak English, and don't know where they're going.

Still, my friends are appalled. They make me promise I'll call them for a ride next time. They've never ridden the bus. I remind them, and myself, this is how people live in big cities. But Louisville is not a big city. It seems like everybody knows your business. Everybody really does know my business. I'm reminded of it every time I venture out. Strangers on the bus sit down to talk to me. Shoppers in the supermarket come up and hug me. Worshippers in church walk up and encourage me. Cops, of all people, stop me while I'm out jogging and tell me how proud they are of my recovery.

I wish that kind of recognition translated to the matter of identification. I never realized how crucial the driver's license is in our society. Now that I don't have one, it seems like everyone is asking for it. I produce my birth certificate, original social security card and numerous photo IDs, but many clerks are unmoved.

"Why don't you have a driver's license?" barks one of them, in front of a bank full of customers staring at a strange standoff.

"Because I just got arrested for drunk driving and had to surrender it in court."

"Oh," she cools down, "You didn't have to go into detail."

"Apparently, I did."

Unfortunately, my kids have to go into detail when their friends ask them why their dad isn't driving. Life in the passenger seat sucks. I duck down when we're passing other parents at practices and games. I'm critical of every phase of my wife's driving. She takes the high road and never brings up the reason why she's driving. Not even when she's happily driving me to recovery meetings, counseling sessions, or the alcohol education classes I have to take to get my driving privileges restored.

There is a bit of good news. Not having a driver's license is turning me into a ripped triathlete again. Every time I need something from the supermarket or hardware store, it gives me another excuse to go running or biking. Nothing I need is more than four miles away. That's only an eight-mile round trip. My end of town looks more like Europe every day with the number of bicycles on the road. I might as well join them.

Taking away my ability to drive has given me the ability to do something I forgot how to do. I have an 11-year old daughter at home and I refuse to let my limitations affect my relationship with her. We take walks. We ride bikes to Dairy Queen. No car stereo. No I-phones. Just a dad and his daughter in deep discussions about life. Important things. Irrelevant things. It was weird at first, with a few complaints. Now she asks to go. She offers up thoughts I never heard before. Old-fashioned parenting still works.

And so does my car. But it's just sitting there in the garage, calling me from time to time. "Hey, c'mon. Just a quick trip to the grocery store. No one will see. No one will know."

Then I think of all those driving-on-suspended-license stories I've done over the years. Camping out in a surveillance van. Catching convicted drunk drivers and others repeatedly unable to resist the temptation. It's not that tough to catch them in the act.

"C'mon John, just this one time," my well-rested Lexus whispers. "There are tons of cars out there like me. Who would know?"

Plenty would know, because I can't go anywhere anymore with a private life. Plus, like an alcoholic taking one drink, if I take that first spin, it won't be the last. That's all I need, to be back in the news.

Now that would be a great story. If I were a cop or an investigative reporter right now, I would be sitting out there, trying to catch me driving.

EAST END HOUSEHUSBAND

The ultimate story of role reversal

I t was one of the funniest things I've ever heard a famous person say. So outrageous to some people, it made the news. So offensive to some women, it still lives in infamy around here. And so much truth involved, it became a popular part of the Louisville vocabulary.

It popped up at the end of a questionnaire being filled out by the high-profile people at a high-profile function. If you could be anything in the world when you return in another life, what would you be? Hall of Fame basketball coach Denny Crum answered, "East End Housewife." He didn't back down when called upon to explain his answer. Tennis or golf in the morning. Lunch at the club. Some shopping or cocktails by the pool in the afternoon. A pretty sweet way to spend your day. Spouses take care of the income. Schools take care of the kids much of the day. The more I thought about it, the more East End Housewives I knew. The more I thought about it, the more I longed for that kind of life and made fun of the people enjoying it.

There's only one problem. Now, I am living that life. Yes, I am an East End Househusband.

Not by choice. When I suddenly went from MVP to untouchably unemployed, my wife picked up a second job to pay the bills and try to keep the house. Learning to be a sober person is tough enough. Learning to be a sober East End Househusband sucks worse than the vacuum.

First, I have to learn how to prepare meals. I got through college with a deep fryer, a sack of potatoes and a fishing pole. I walked down to the river, caught a couple of smallmouth bass and fried 'em up with the sliced taters. I need to do a little better than that now.

I have to make beds. I got a start on that in rehab when they ordered that we make our beds to specific standards or be fined a buck. A dollar is a terrible thing to waste because a bedspread is touching the floor.

I do all the wash now. I never realized how much clothing a sixth grade girl goes through in one day. I've always been anal about the way my wash is done, so this is not a big burden.

I do all the house cleaning. I used to think home maintenance chores like mowing and trimming were time-consuming. This is ridiculous. How many times do the floors and sinks need scrubbing?

Truth is, I don't have to do any of this stuff. There is no gun to my head. The biggest challenge I face is living up to the standards I expected when I was the breadwinner. So I run a tight ship. I make sure dinner is ready the second my family walks through the door. I remember how valuable my free time was when I was working all day. But I feel like the catcher in a baseball game. He's not noticed for catching all the balls and making all the calls. No one says a thing until he drops the ball.

From meals to homework, house maintenance to relationship maintenance, being an East End Househusband is far more difficult than I imagined. But I had a feeling that would be the case. What I didn't expect is much harder to define. I'm having a difficult time finding value in my role here, holding down the fort and the troops. I know that Jesus was pretty clear about the importance of this role in the family unit. That's why many Christians still look down on dual-income families. But I'm discovering I worked way too long, way too hard, and put way too much value in my job.

I've heard marriage experts say the most important thing to a woman is to feel loved, while the most important thing to a man is to feel respected. And most men draw that respect from their jobs. I think we've got it all wrong. But that's just another way that my mind is wired wrong.

I just want to get a high five when my meals are on time, or a pat on the back after I've saved money at the supermarket. No tennis here. No golf. No lunches at a restaurant. Not even fast food. No shopping. No poolside cocktails. But I do have to clean our pool a lot so my working wife has a place to chill with the East End Housewives out here in my neighborhood.

JUDGMENT DAY

When the reporter becomes the defendant, it isn't pretty.

A nother card in the mail from my daughter. That's eight days in a row. This one is well-timed and prophetic, because I'm going to court to plead guilty today.

Her card reads, "The best thing you can do to all of the hotshots determining your case is kill them with kindness. Easier said than done but I think you've done a good job of it so far."

A college sophomore isn't supposed to be encouraging her dad before his court sentencing. A mature adult is supposed to be there for a troubled teen when she trips up. But Kelsey never trips up, despite details in her cards of all the people tripping up around her.

"One guy who had been coming to church and even got baptized and stuff got arrested this past week for drug trafficking. He'll most likely be in jail for five to seven years."

My daughter is more mature at 19 than I am at 48. She's worried about me, so I find a card in my mailbox every day.

"I don't know why you think these external things would make me feel shame over you in any way. I see what everyone else doesn't—a sincere heart, and it's the internal things that count. If people bad-mouth you the rest of your life, it wouldn't change how I think of you."

She ends this note with a verse from scripture. "Anyone who trusts in Him will never be put to shame. Romans 10:11."

But shame is dripping off of me as I sit in the front row of Bullitt County District Court. The place is packed. Other than the attorneys, I'm the only person in a suit. If majority rules, the dress code here appears to be multiple lip, nose and tongue studs. Tattoos are required, not optional. Truth is, I may dress differently, but I'm no better than anyone here. I used to think I was. I'm being painfully humbled once again. In fact, karma is coming at me from all angles. On the way in to this courtroom, I saw one of the many police officers who've been targets of my stories. Cops driving 90 miles an hour to get to Victoria's Secret to buy pink panties. Cops beating a man trying to get a U-Haul to his tornado-leveled home with rain on the way. Cops driving past guys clearly dealing drugs. Cops using Tasers on people pushing a lawn mower down the street or riding a bike with a flat tire.

They're all getting the last laugh now.

The prosecutor who dished out this deal came from another office where I routinely did stories critical of their performance. The county I'm in now is the one I poked the most fun of as a journalist, from its twice-weekly meth lab busts to its twice-yearly military gun show where a Third World country-sized arsenal of machine guns are emptied on unsuspecting refrigerators and washing machines. But now the sights on the scopes of Bullitt County justice are aimed at me.

I sit in the front row so I don't have to stare back at the stares. In the jumbled buzz of people talking about me, some are wondering what case I'm covering. But most of them know exactly why I'm here. There are 6,000 arrests in Kentucky every year for DUI–2nd offense. Only one made the local news this year. And it looks like they're trying to make an example out of the defendant.

Between counseling sessions and meetings I attend, I've met about 15 people so far who've been sentenced for the same offense, with the same "aggravator" circumstances as mine. None of them checked themselves into rehab like I did. And the most serious punishment any of them received was seven days of home incarceration. So, I'm shocked when I learn I'm getting socked with 28 days of home incarceration, along with the typical one-year loss of license, one year of alcohol education classes, and $1,000 in court costs. By my math, that means I will wind up spending one month in rehab and one month in home incarceration, while others I've met in the same boat did one week at home, max.

Just about the time I can't feel any sorrier for myself, an old man walks up to me, in front of everyone, before court is set to begin.

"Excuse me; you're John Boel, right?"

"Yes, sir," I respond, extending my hand.

But this is no fan. He looks down, refusing to shake my hand. It looks like he wants to spit on it in disgust.

"I'm George Miller's father . . ." he begins. I have no idea who George Miller is. The rest of his rant is a blur, as he begins taunting and ripping me. I figure this must be the relative of a victim of drunken driving, so I sit there and take every lash of his wordy whip. When he finally walks away, my head is swimming. The judge will be much easier on me than he just was.

"Who was that?" my stunned wife asks.

I have no idea. I've done a lot of stories in 22 years here. Clearly, the karma continues to flow. It's only after I get home and do a little research that I realize what triggered that confrontation. George Miller killed two people in a drunken driving crash. He was sentenced to 20 years in prison after pleading guilty to manslaughter and wanton endangerment. He's been sitting in prison for seven years already. It's a case I covered, and I remember having a tearful exchange during an interview with the mother of one of the victims. How ashamed she must be of me right now.

The two guys killed in that crash had been out in the street after being involved in their own fender bender. The drunken driver with slow reaction time came along and hit them. Now I understand the old man's rant. In my condition, I could have done the same thing. I could have been sent to prison for 20 years or more. Suddenly, 28 days of home incarceration doesn't seem so bad.

When I get home and check the mailbox, sure enough, there's card number nine.

"But as for you, be strong and do not give up, for your work will be rewarded. 2 Chronicles 15:7."

I've already been rewarded. I have a 19 year old with more wisdom, more faith and more maturity than I've ever had. Yes, I did something wrong. But I did something right, as well. I raised a little girl who is now raising her father up out of the depths of despair.

"For the sake of Christ then, I am content with weaknesses, insults, hardships, persecutions and calamities. For when I am weak, then I am strong. 2 Corinthians 12:10."

GROUNDED

Valuing life by being forced to watch it go by

I never got grounded as a kid. Only got spanked once, and that was for good reason. My neighbor and I took apart a little girl's doll stroller and rebuilt it into a go-cart. I had no idea she was poor and it was her only Christmas present.

But here I am, with a GPS device the size of a small camera fastened to a thick band that wraps around my ankle. I wear shorts around the house year 'round, but I've been wearing sweat pants and jeans so my 11-year-old daughter doesn't see it. It was hard enough sitting her down and explaining why dad spent the night in jail. Why he wouldn't be able to drive for a year. Why he had to go away for a month to try to get better. And why he had been fired from the job she knows he loved. Now I'm trying to explain to the middle-school class president why I won't be at her school functions and softball and field hockey practices and games for awhile.

"When you do something wrong, you have to suffer the penalty. I went in and pleaded guilty and accepted my punishment. Basically, I'm being grounded for a few weeks."

"You mean, like, house arrest?"

How does she know what that is? I was careful not to use the term "home incarceration." Maybe I didn't say it that way because "grounded" doesn't sound so bad.

"Yes, honey, that's what it's called. I can't leave the house."

After a brutally cold winter and spring, my first day of home incarceration blooms into 74 beautiful, sunny degrees. The first great day of the year. The April Fool's joke is on me. But there's a valuable lesson to be learned as I sit here looking out the window. If I were outside enjoying this weather, I wouldn't be enjoying it. I would be furiously pedaling my bike or trying to trick fish into biting. I wouldn't hear how loud and happy the birds are. I wouldn't see how powerful the purple lilacs and redbud trees are right now. Worst of all, I wouldn't miss any of it.

Every other year, on a Saturday like this, I was at Keeneland Race Course. My face was buried in the handicapping form or I was standing in the long beer line. Watching it on TV now, I can't take my eyes off the vibrant dogwoods and the chiseled Thoroughbreds.

The only thing more challenging than triathlon training is triathlon training indoors with a clunky, cumbersome GPS device flopping around on my leg. Thick socks and duct tape keep it fairly stationary on the exercise bike. But running is another story. To offset and balance out this unusual ankle weight I have on my right leg, I tape a couple of large flashlight batteries to my left ankle. Duct tape never ceases to amaze. The treadmill never knows the difference.

I'm not allowed to attend a house of God while on house

arrest. Not even on Easter. So, when my wife and daughter leave for church, I watch the previous week's sermon at my church on my computer. Then I flip on the TV and scroll through the TV evangelists I used to make fun of. Joel Osteen is one of the preachers I thought was smarmy. Now that I'm forced to watch him, I realize that's just one more thing I had totally wrong. His message today is on "labels." I'm not who people say I am. I am who God says I am. My sin is not my identity. Nothing that has happened in my past has to keep me from my destiny. I need to tear off the old labels and sew on some new ones. I'm redeemed, restored and rebuilt. He's right. From rehab, to group counseling, to 12-step meetings, to struggling friends, I feel like I've already helped more people than I did over decades of being a journalist. In-home church isn't so bad after all. Best part is, I can get on my knees, pray out loud and cry out loud, and nobody is looking at me.

I don't know what happens if I stray beyond the invisible home incarceration perimeter encircling me. Will my ankle device start blinking? Will the phone ring? Will cops be dispatched? The H.I.P. supervisor says the satellite-monitored perimeter is roughly the circumference of my house, so I can step out a few feet on the front porch or back deck. Thankfully, I'm not one of the dogs in my neighborhood that gets zapped in the neck when he strays out of his invisibly fenced yard. My dog is always searching for a way to break out of her fenced-in backyard. Now I understand why.

As I sit here, I can't stop thinking about all the hours

done my share of stories on "things gone wrong" in jails. But for my last day, a jail deputy arranges to make sure I can be freed at 5 A.M.

I arrive early. It's a busy time at the Bullitt County jail. Meth dealers and drunk drivers are going through the same booking process I went through six months ago here. One of the workers stops what he's doing and comes out to greet me. He acts like he knows me. Turns out he does. He was present at some of the animal control investigations I did back in the mid-1990s.

He apologizes for the trouble he's having disassembling the black box around my right ankle. It doesn't look like a chainsaw and sledgehammer could get this thing off. But, finally, the GPS monitor falls into pieces. Before I can dash out, he looks me in the eye and asks me how I'm doing. I can tell he's not just making small talk. He really cares. Much like leaving the rehab van at the airport, it's one of those moments I'm going to remember for the rest of my life. A period of darkness is ending. It's time to move into the light again. People don't realize the difference they can make by taking some time to probe and encourage others. It seems like the most important events in my life happen at the most insignificant moments. This time, it's a busy overnight jailer sending me out the door with a feeling of support, optimism and opportunity.

I'm not being watched by satellite anymore, but God is monitoring my every move. Others are watching me closely, too. I can hear their comments in the crowd as I make my way toward the starting line in Louisville.

"Isn't that the TV guy?"

"Hey, there's John Boel."

This is a great time to be wearing an I-pod. Time to crank up the AC/DC. I don't want to fixate on what others are saying about me today. I want to focus on freedom and fitness and life.

No one here will take my money. Registration for the race has been cut off. They capped it at 15,000 entries. I don't care. I'm running it anyway. I paid the entry fees while giving them great race coverage exposure for over a decade, so they owe me.

When my crafty dog is able to escape from the house, she runs as fast and as long as she can until she drops. Now I know why. There's something about captivity that makes me want to dash farther and faster than I've ever run before. But there has also been a change inside me. That serenity prayer I repeated a dozen times a day in rehab is making me want to savor every step of this event.

"Lord, grant me the serenity to accept the things I cannot change, the courage to change the things I can, and the wisdom to know the difference."

As I shuffle slowly toward the start with the masses, I don't even hear the cannon. There is something divine and spiritual about the start of every race I have ever entered. It's always at daybreak on one of God's beautiful mornings. I always think of how blessed I am to be able to attempt this foot race or triathlon, while my sister and so many others can't even try. But today, I can't get the serenity prayer out of my mind. Who knows how fast my legs are churning?

My mind is racing. Recounting all of the things "I cannot change" about my life.

I lost a lot when I tried to drive home that day. I lost a job that I adored and poured myself into for 22 years. I lost a work family that I spent more hours with each day than my own family. I lost my freedom for a while. I lost the ability to drive for a year. I lost the respect I worked decades to build. I lost the ability to look at myself in the mirror. And I lost my mind while I was losing to addiction.

All of those things ran away from me as fast as some of the runners blowing by me already at mile marker four. That's okay. Let 'em go. The race is not over. While I lost a step as an athlete and I lost a lot as an alcoholic, I found much more in my program of recovery.

I found human beings capable of things I never knew existed. People at the best and worst times of their lives dropping everything to help wretches like me. I found a clear, intelligent, re-wired brain in there somewhere. I found a relationship with my family that was never allowed to blossom before. I always made sure I denied it water or warmth at just the right time. Or I just smashed it with my boot. My wife says she's the happiest she's ever been. My 11 year old looks at me like she adores me. I feel like her father, her friend and an attractive boy in her class, all at the same time. The "courage to change the things I can" sounds easier than it really is. It takes hard, humbling work to make change happen.

That's how I find strength in life. In this race, I need to pop another carbohydrate gel because my leg strength is already fading at mile marker eight. This is a valuable endurance lesson. Training exclusively on a treadmill for the entire month leading up to a race doesn't cut it. My muscles forgot what a real road feels like. Real streets don't spin round and round on their own beneath you.

Up ahead, a bunch of college kids are out on the curb. All holding beers. Already drunk. That was me. A roar from the crowd erupts as a passing runner grabs a beer and chugs it. That was me, too.

Little kids are passing me now at mile marker 11. That's okay, too. It reminds me of the little boy who wet himself during my live interview. I wonder if he is still running. I wonder if I'm going to make it to the finish before I have to go in my own shorts. Glancing at my watch, I can't believe I used to be able to average seven-minute miles in this race. Now I'm struggling to average eights.

There's a wonderful feeling that enters your body when you get into the final mile of a race. You know you're going to make it. You know the pain is almost over. I just ran past the spot where I collapsed in my own vomit, with failing vital signs, and had to be rushed to the hospital during the Ironman Triathlon a couple of years ago. I know now that had to be an alcohol-related crash. Surprising how efficiently my body engine is running, now that I've been sober six months.

The finish line looms ahead. What a struggle it was to get here in so many ways. I'm tired of struggling. It seems like every hour of every day is a struggle. Addiction. Unemployment. Stigma. Depression. For most of these people around me, sprinting or stumbling down the home stretch, the finish line marks a real end of something. For the 20 million people like me in this country struggling with addiction, it's never really over. There is no finish line. But I'm going to celebrate anyway. My race streak is alive. My sobriety streak is alive. And I am more alive than ever.

The last left turn reveals a gauntlet of deafening spectators lining the home stretch. Finish strong. But I'm not trying to impress anybody today. I keep thinking of the Bible verse my daughter sent me for encouragement recently, ". . . let us also lay aside every weight and sin which clings so closely, and let us run with endurance the race that is set before us . . ."

So much weight. So much sin. So many races to conquer in our lives. But what a wonderful feeling, whether that endurance race is on a road, or on the road to recovery.

On my way to the car, a woman stops me.

"John Boel! Where have you been? Could I please have your autograph?"

My autograph? You've got to be kidding. I'm not Ron Burgundy anymore. I'm not one of the Kenyans who dominated this race. I always despised signing autographs for people. I didn't know why. I realize now it's because I wasn't very proud of myself. Reputation is what you are when everyone is looking. Character is what you are when no one is looking.

But as I stand there sweating and stinking, the more I think about it, I realize my name does mean something now. For the first time in a long time, my signature has value. My recovery has value. My life has value. This woman doesn't know why, but I do.

"You know what, ma'am? Give me something to write on. I'd love to sign something for you."

UNSCRIPTED MOMENT

Preach what you practice.

I t's Ironman week. I'm booked on a bunch of radio shows to talk about the insane day of swimming, biking and running, as thousands of athletes arrive in Louisville from 28 different countries and 48 states to give it a try.

I'm the local expert on the 140-mile-long triathlon because I do it every year. But this year is going to different. I've been sober for almost ten months, lost 45 pounds, and joblessness gives me much more time to train. I always wanted to be like the professional triathletes who are paid by a sponsor to train all day. But the only sponsor I have is in my 12-step recovery program. He doesn't pay. If anything, I should be paying him.

As a journalist, I was a terrible interviewer. I'm not much better when I'm the person being interviewed. But this one seems to be going well. Perhaps that's because I'm on the Terry Meiners radio show.

Terry is a longtime friend. He knows what I'm going through because he has witnessed struggles with addiction. He knows when I need someone to talk to, and he knows when I need to silently watch football with a buddy. We can talk about anything, on or off the air. But when he asks me about my battle with alcoholism, in the middle of a drive-time discussion about the upcoming Ironman Triathlon, it stops me cold. A thousand thoughts shoot through my mind in a thousandth of a second. I decide to take a risk. I decide to tell the disturbing story of what I was doing one year ago this week.

Last year, seven days before the Ironman, I realized I was drinking almost daily. Not always drunk. But almost always something right before bed. I had never experienced this before and I was scared, especially with a grueling physical endurance test coming up in one week. When I learned the forecast called for a race day high of 96 degrees, I vowed to stop drinking for one week. A temporary purge of poison. I knew this was a serious situation. People die attempting the Ironman. Sober people.

But it was a beautiful weekend, so I drank. On Monday, I was feeling sorry for myself again, working 3:30 in the morning to 6 at night, so I drank. Tuesday, Wednesday and Thursday rolled by. Same thing. On Friday, I registered for the race, got my gear together, and then begged myself to relax and abstain. My family was gone for the night. I bought a 12-pack. Beer, not Gatorade. I drank the 12-pack of beer, alone in front of the TV, on the Friday night before the Ironman Triathlon. I could not stop drinking for one night, despite a daunting 140 miles of pain in 96-degree heat hanging over my head. The final excuse that trickled out of my brain: at least it's Lite beer.

As I vomited for hours on a cot in the medical unit, watching bags of IV pour into my parched and polluted body, after my slowest Ironman ever, I blamed my poor performance on the heat.

In disbelief, Terry follows up, "You and I have spent a lot of time together. I'm no dope. I'm pretty perceptive. How was I oblivious to all this?" That's just it. We're good at keeping secrets, no matter how debilitating. We pull off amazing feats after polishing off a 12-pack.

I hang up the telephone. I can't believe what I just publicly confessed. One minute later, my phone starts ringing. My Facebook fills. Emails erupt. They're from people who need help. Or they're from people who know someone who needs help. They don't know what to do, but they know they just heard the same disturbing stuff they're trying to deal with in their own lives. Every message is different. But every message is really the same.

"Mr Boel, I watched you a number of times when I lived in Louisville. Who would have known we shared so much in common. I, like you, thought I hid my disease because I tried my best to stay active and fit. Until the last year or two, it got the best of me . . ."

"I listened to your pre-race interview with Terry, John, and wanted to thank you for putting your story out there. It gave me a lot to think about, in terms of my own drinking and the way your earlier patterns parallel mine now. Your interview has given me a lot to think about . . ."

"To hear you today gives me hope, Mr. Boel. I heard every word you were saying and I am at that point in my life. I hide mine and it has caused me to move out and find support at a 12-step program. You give me hope . . ."

One of the calls to my home is from a police officer. One of the calls is from one of my former rivals in TV news. We never spoke before. Now we're swapping stories for an hour. He's been battling alcoholism for a long time and can't string together any sustained sobriety. I had no idea.

My wife walks by and mutters the same thing I'm thinking. "If you had told me a few years ago that you would be sitting here for hours helping other people, I would have never believed it."

She's right. Even when I was helping others as a journalist, I was more concerned about the ratings, the next assignment, or the next drink.

As the messages pile up, it's becoming painfully clear there are many more people around me struggling with this disease than I ever imagined. There are more than 300 recovery meetings per week in Louisville, just that I know of. Come to think of it, there are always newcomers at every one I attend. So many people hurting. So many more sufferers out there not being reached by the existing recovery programs. One brief story on one radio station has triggered an avalanche of pleas for help.

One last email before bed:

"I believe it was a God thing that had me tune to 840 while driving down the road to hear your story . . ."

The email exchange with this young man finds he too suffered DUI problems and thoughts of suicide. We have a lot in common. Then I learn his sobriety birthday is the day after mine.

He's right. There's no way that was a coincidence. Whether it was "a God thing" or not, I don't know. But I'm helping others. And they're helping me. That's the way the program is supposed to work. If baring and sharing my fame-to-shame story and my own rough road through recovery can help even one person stay sober and stay alive, it will give my life new purpose.

Recovery is hard. A triathlon is easy. A real Ironman finishes both.